MW00387609

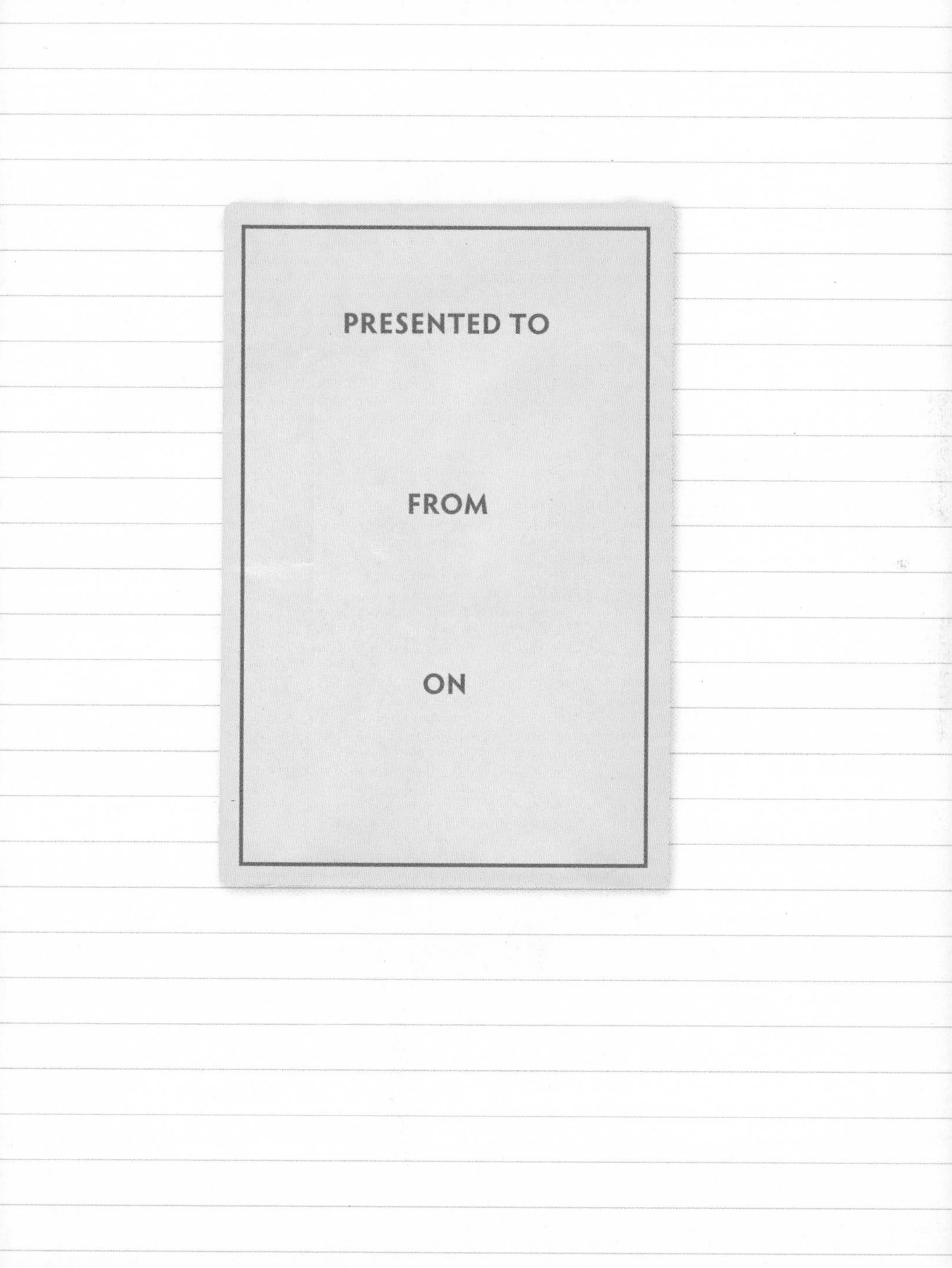
PRESENTED TO
FROM
ON

Children's
Warbler

52 Devotions & Prayers for Women

CALLED *to pray*

Marsha DuCille

Tyndale House Publishers
Carol Stream, Illinois

Living Expressions invites you to explore God's Word in a way that is refreshing to the spirit and restorative to the soul.

Visit Tyndale online at tyndale.com.

Visit CALLED at calledinc.com.

CALLED to Pray: 52 Devotions & Prayers for Women

Designed by Libby Dykstra

For information about special discounts for bulk purchases, please contact Tyndale House Publishers at csresponse@tyndale.com, or call 1-800-323-9400.

ISBN 978-1-4964-3594-1

Printed in China

27 26 25 24 23 22 21
7 6 5 4 3 2 1

Yellow-throated Warbler

CONTENTS

INTRODUCTION

PRAYER IS LESS COMPLICATED than many think. Oddly, some religions claim that it requires certain clothing, specific chants, a particular time of day, or a shower. *(Yes, a shower!)* But prayer—our conversation with God—is about building an authentic relationship. It can happen anywhere and at any time; and there's no extra credit for eloquent words or lengthy speeches.

Some people pray in writing and through songs, while others pray in their hearts or out loud. Whatever your approach, *CALLED to Pray* will help you connect with God in an effective and gratifying way.

Throughout this beautiful journal book, you'll find *fifty-two devotions* that guide you into a more meaningful prayer life. The topics cover real-life issues that impact real-life women—because our lives have many ups and downs. There are also *fifty-two declarations* and *fifty-two prayers* to echo the deepest sentiments of your heart.

God is calling you into a closer relationship with him. Prayers don't have to be complicated, so make yours whatever you need them to be.

~Marsha DuCille

1. The Meaning

For Understanding Prayer

Band-tailed Pigeon

SIMPLY PUT, PRAYER IS A TWO-WAY CONVERSATION between you and God. It's an all-purpose connection to a Father who yearns for a relationship with you. The Lord said, "Come to me with your ears wide open. Listen, and you will find life. I will make an everlasting covenant with you. I will give you . . . unfailing love" (Isaiah 55:3).

You'll find 222 prayers in the King James Bible. The mere volume can seem quite daunting. But if anything, let the vastness inspire you to make your prayer talks more *personal*, more *creative*, more *whatever* you need them to be.

Jesus prayed early in the morning, while it was still dark; the psalmists prayed through songs and poetry; and Hannah prayed silently—through the hidden petitions of her heart.

In your conversations with God, you'll find friendship, a warrior's battlefield, and complete serenity. The Lord says, "Call to me and I will answer you and tell you great and unsearchable things" (Jeremiah 33:3, NIV).

STRENGTH IN THE WORD

You will pray to him,
and he will hear you.

JOB 22:27

TODAY I DECLARE

The Lord is my
all-purpose friend.

PRAYERFUL THOUGHTS

Dear Lord,

Open the windows of heaven, so you may always hear my voice. Walk and talk with me—as you did with Adam—in the coolness of the day. Tell me that you're listening, my ever-faithful God.

Open my ears to your instruction; help me know it's you I hear. Take my hand, dear heavenly Father, and guide me into a stronger relationship with you.

In Jesus' name, amen.

* KEEPSAKE

"Prayer is a two-way conversation."

2. Look Around

For Greater Faith

MY FAITH HAS AN UNFAIR ADVANTAGE—because I've seen what others have to blindly believe. At the age of nine, I slipped into a coma, and my doctor said that I was headed toward death. I didn't know much about God, but while comatose, I experienced something supernatural and miraculous. *Supernatural* because I had a divine encounter; *miraculous* because I'm still here.

Based on what I saw, I know—with certainty—that God is real. This certitude has given me the advantage of knowing that a real God hears my prayers. But each of us can have greater faith simply by looking around. The psalmist wrote: "The heavens proclaim the glory of God. The skies display his craftsmanship. Day after day they continue to speak; night after night they make him known" (Psalm 19:1-2).

Taking a prayer walk (on the beach, along a trail, or up a mountain) is a wonderful way to "see" God. Surrounded by the beauty of his creation, you'll be assured that God is real.

STRENGTH IN THE WORD

Through everything God made, [you] can clearly see his invisible qualities.

ROMANS 1:20

TODAY I DECLARE

I can see God if I look.

PRAYERFUL THOUGHTS

Dear Lord,

When my faith grows weak, please show me that you're real. Some days, I need to know that you're not a figment of my imagination. Reveal your invisible hand in both the spectacular and small—the wave of the ocean, the sunset in the sky, the rainbow after the rain, and the brush of the wind.

Please awaken my senses and wipe away my doubts.

In Jesus' name, amen.

KEEPSAKE

"I know—with certainty—that God is real."

3. You Are Not Alone

For Enduring Hardship

IN 1979, MOTHER TERESA WROTE these doleful words to her spiritual confidant, Reverend Michael van der Peet: "Jesus has a very special love for you. . . . As for me—the silence and the emptiness is so great that I look and do not see, listen and do not hear. . . . The tongue moves [in prayer] but does not speak."

We may never know what caused Mother Teresa to cry out, but it's clear that she felt alone. I wish I could tell you that loving God takes away all of our hardships, but we both know that isn't true. On the cross, "Jesus called out with a loud voice, '*Eli, Eli, lema sabachthani?*' which means 'My God, my God, why have you abandoned me?'" (Matthew 27:46).

Your struggles will sometimes make you *feel* alone and forgotten, but God is an ever-present Father. He always walks *before you* (to make a way); walks *beside you* (to keep you strong); and walks *behind you* (to catch you if you fall).

STRENGTH IN THE WORD

He will neither fail you nor abandon you.

DEUTERONOMY 31:6

TODAY I DECLARE

Through every peak and valley, God is with me.

PRAYERFUL THOUGHTS

Dear Lord,

In my struggles, I feel alone. At times, I even question if you care. But I know that you are faithful and loving—attentive and loyal. You are the God who never forsakes me.

Please help me to see you in this darkness, and remind me that these feelings don't reflect what is true. Wrap me in the blanket of your presence.

In Jesus' name, amen.

KEEPSAKE

"God is an ever-present Father."

4. Go Ahead & Ask

For Boldness

WHEN WAS THE LAST TIME you asked God for something big? I mean for something far beyond what you thought was probable or deserving? Too often, Christians pray for the minimum. We pray for strength *for the day* and provision *for a bill*. But what if we prayed with boldness? Not for the minimum, but for the maximum—infinitely more than what we *usually* ask or think (Ephesians 3:20).

God has given us permission to boldly come before his throne (Hebrews 4:16). By faith, we can receive *complete* healing and *all-encompassing* blessings, and *every* mountain can be moved. Jesus told his disciples, "You don't have enough faith. . . . I tell you the truth, if you had faith even as small as a mustard seed, you could say to this mountain, 'Move from here to there,' and it would move. Nothing would be impossible" (Matthew 17:20).

So go ahead and ask the Lord for your biggest, most audacious, *I don't deserve this* desire. He's daring you to pray with bold faith.

STRENGTH IN THE WORD

May God pass on to you and your descendants the blessings he promised to Abraham.

GENESIS 28:4

TODAY I DECLARE

The boldness of my faith is rooted in the power of my God.

PRAYERFUL THOUGHTS

Dear Lord,

It's hard to imagine that my faith has immeasurable power, but I choose to believe your Word and boldly pray:

> Let your maximum favor and provision fall upon every area of my life. Not only for today—but for every day—and upon the descendants who come after me. I boldly ask that you make *blessed* my first name and *highly favored* my last.

In Jesus' name, amen.

KEEPSAKE

"Boldly come before his throne."

5. Someone Else

For Unsaved Loved Ones

Prairie Starling

SHARING THE GOSPEL IS TOUGH, especially when it comes to reaching our loved ones. These folks know all about our messy pasts; and some seem to specialize in examining our flaws. In fact, Jesus observed that even "a prophet has little honor in his hometown, among his relatives, on the streets he played in as a child" (Mark 6:4, MSG).

Consequently, *prayer* is the only way you'll be able to reach certain loved ones—because some won't be able to receive the Good News through you. Mark 6 reports that Jesus couldn't do much in his hometown. "He's just a carpenter," people said (Mark 6:3, MSG). And "even his brothers didn't believe in him" (John 7:5).

When it comes to winning souls for the Lord, we must remember that we're in this race together. Though you, personally, might not reach your sister or friend, you can pray for God to send someone else. "Pray to the Lord who is in charge of the harvest; ask him to send more workers into his fields" (Matthew 9:38).

STRENGTH IN THE WORD

Believe in the Lord Jesus and you will be saved, along with everyone in your household.

ACTS 16:31

TODAY I DECLARE

My loved ones will be saved.

PRAYERFUL THOUGHTS

Dear Lord,

I plead the blood of Jesus over ______________'s life. Even before the creation of the world, you loved ________________.

Please touch his/her heart, O Lord. Prepare it for one of your special messengers. Send someone who can minister to his/her struggles, doubts, and needs.

Let your truth prevail, and may the bondage of sin be broken.

In Jesus' name, amen.

* KEEPSAKE

"We're in this race together."

6. Just Sing

For Praying through Songs

DO YOU KNOW that singing is a type of prayer? The book of Psalms is comprised of 150 prayer-songs, and scholars have counted at least 30 others throughout the Bible. If we define prayer as our conversations with God, it makes sense that singing would qualify.

After Paul and Silas were beaten and thrown into prison, they prayed through hymns. Acts 16 states, "At midnight Paul and Silas praying, were singing hymns to God . . . and suddenly a great earthquake came, so that the foundations of the prison were shaken, . . . all the doors [were opened], and . . . the bands were loosed" (verses 25-26, YLT).

Oh, yes. Prayer-songs did all of that!

You don't need the most majestic voice to pray through melodies. God filters your voice through the sincerity and intentions of your heart. Psalm 95:1 instructs, "Sing to the LORD!" That is, sing no matter how good or bad you sound. Serenade God through hymns, psalms, or made-up tunes that communicate whatever is in your heart.

▸◂ STRENGTH IN THE WORD

Come, let us sing to the LORD!

PSALM 95:1

◂▸ TODAY I DECLARE

Heaven awaits the songs
of my heart.

PRAYERFUL THOUGHTS

Dear Lord,

I lift my voice to sing your praises; I sing these melodies to draw closer to you. May the sounds from my heart bring you joy; may you hear my adoration and heartfelt love.

Though my voice is weak and far from perfect, your grace listens and covers the flaws. Yes, I will sing because you are worthy; I will sing unto you because you are my God.

In Jesus' name, amen.

7. Jesus

For Praying His Name

DURING A VERY TOUGH SEASON, I sat in my car and a swarm of emotions hit me: *disappointment, hopelessness, regret.* They all came at once. With tears streaming down my face, I closed my eyes and slowly whispered, "*Jesus.*" Instantly, something came over me. It was like a morphine shot that subdued the pain. So I said it again, "*Jesus.*" And then again, "*Jesus.*" I don't know how many times I called his name; but with that simple prayer, I felt indescribable comfort and relief.

There's power in the name of Jesus. His name, alone, is burden removing and hope restoring. Philippians 2 proclaims, "God made his name greater than every other name so that every knee will bow to the name of Jesus" (verses 9-10, NCV). That means *hopelessness* and *pain* must bow; *regret* and *worry* must bow; *every single burden* must bow.

So what should you do when you feel lost and alone? In the words of Martha Munizzi's song, "When you don't know what else to pray . . . say the name."

STRENGTH IN THE WORD

Everyone who calls on the name of the LORD will be saved.

ROMANS 10:13

TODAY I DECLARE

Jesus is my constant prayer.

PRAYERFUL THOUGHTS

Dear Lord,

Your name is a strong tower. The righteous run to it and find safety. With the simple utterance of your name, no burden can stand. Chains of bondage are broken; and every aching sore is soothed.

Jesus, I pray over my spirit, mind, and body. *Jesus*, I pray over every single area of my life. When it's hard to face the day—and I don't know what to pray—I'll say your name.

In Jesus' name, amen.

KEEPSAKE

"There's power in the name of Jesus."

8. His Preferred Way

For Healing

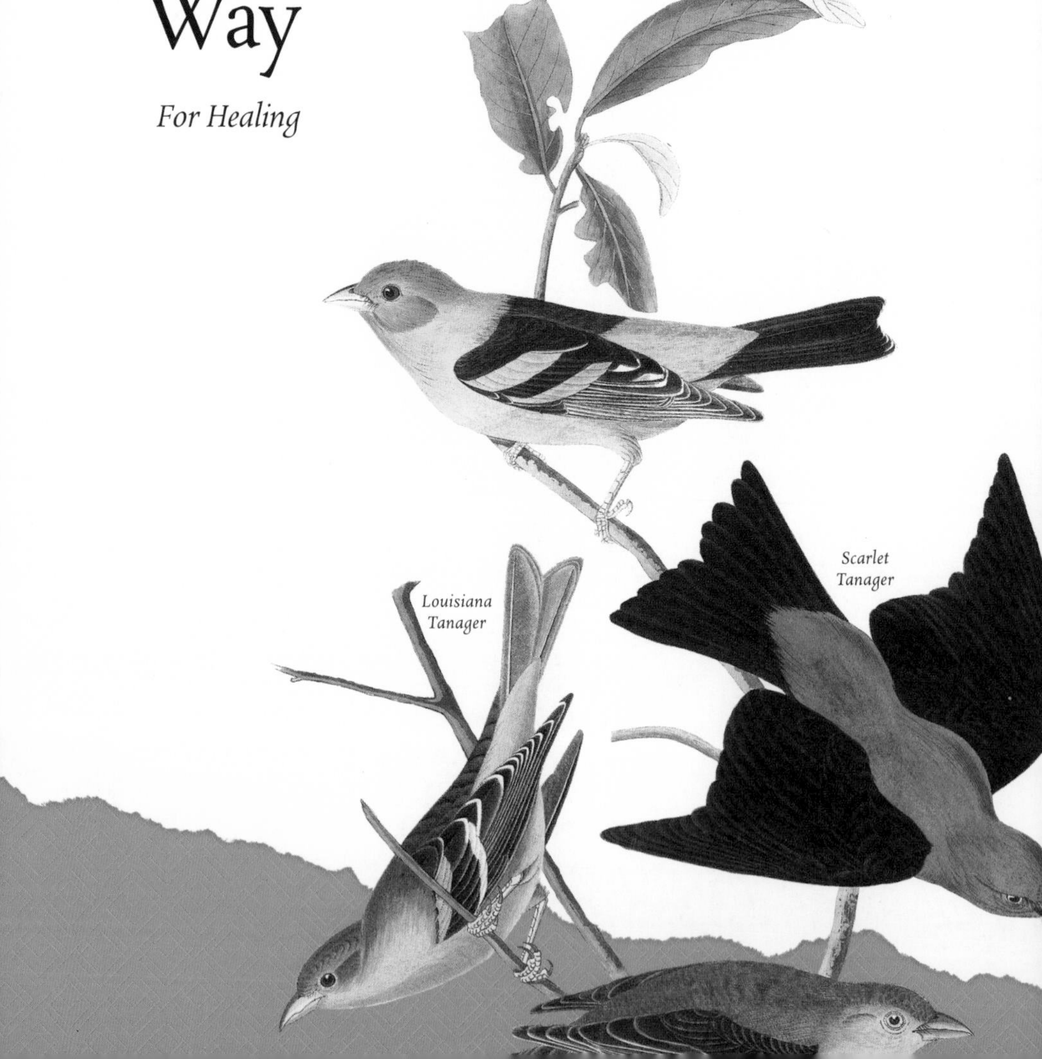

WHEN IT COMES TO HEALING, many of us have our preferences. And to some extent, that's okay. But we can't pray, "Lord, *heal my marriage* (but I'm not willing to change); *heal my body* (but I'm still smoking and eating what I want); *heal my finances* (but I'm not downsizing or giving up this car)." Healing doesn't work that way.

God sometimes works through the undesired and unexpected. In 2 Kings 5, Naaman protested being healed in the Jordan River, but that was God's preferred way (verses 11-15). Moreover, Jesus healed the blind using *three* different methods: In Jericho, he simply spoke the words (Mark 10:52); in Jerusalem, he made mud with saliva (John 9:6); and in Bethsaida, he spat directly on the blind man's eyes (Mark 8:23).

When you pray, God can heal whatever aspect of your life is aching. But you'll have to receive your healing using *his* methods, under *his* conditions, and through *his* preferred way.

STRENGTH IN THE WORD

I am the LORD who heals you.

EXODUS 15:26

TODAY I DECLARE

Because of Christ, healing and wholeness belong to me.

PRAYERFUL THOUGHTS

Dear Lord,

Thank you for being a God who heals and a God who cares. Today, I submit to you everything that is aching in my life, and I yield to your preferred methods.

Please heal my *body*, and heal my *mind*.

Heal my *finances*, and heal my *relationships*.

Please reveal which actions I must take—to receive healing.

In Jesus' name, amen.

KEEPSAKE

"God works through the undesired and unexpected."

9. High Costs

For Unnecessary Battles

HAVE YOU HEARD of a *Pyrrhic victory*? It's a victory that comes at such a debilitating cost, it's essentially a defeat. The term originally referred to the Greek general Pyrrhus of Epirus. In the third century BC, he battled the Roman Empire and won. But in the process of fighting, Pyrrhus lost his best officers and friends.

There's no doubt that some battles are necessary, but I'd venture to say that most are not. For instance, the second someone mentions politics, I know that I'd better pray—*because some silly battle is about to start!* And you probably have a "way-too-sensitive" hot button that's provoked by something (or someone) else.

Through prayer, God teaches us when and how to chill. Second Timothy 2:23-24 instructs us, "Refuse to get involved in inane discussions; they always end up in fights. God's servant must not be argumentative, but a gentle listener and a teacher who keeps cool" (MSG).

Therefore, *pray* when you're lured into foolish battles—because losing your peace and reputation are too high a cost.

STRENGTH IN THE WORD

Pray that you will not give in to temptation.

LUKE 22:40

TODAY I DECLARE

I'll count the costs.

PRAYERFUL THOUGHTS

Dear Lord,

I've had many Pyrrhic victories—wins that weren't worth the fight. But now I'm asking that you remove all that nonsense from my life.

Please cool down my hot buttons, O Lord, and reshape me into a person who isn't provoked. Give me ears that can listen to anything without hopping into the flames of a fight.

Help me count the cost of potential battles—and teach me when and how to chill.

In Jesus' name, amen.

KEEPSAKE

"God teaches us when and how to chill."

10. Good vs. Best

For Waiting on God

HAVE YOU HEARD of Club 33? The waiting list for this high-priced club at Disneyland is up to *fourteen years*. Yes, folks wait *over a decade* to schmooze with Mickey Mouse.

Daily, we wait for things that (in the grand scheme of life) aren't important: at Starbucks, the DMV, and Black Friday—*to name a few*. But when it comes to waiting on God, our patience often runs thin. Hastily, we settle for less or completely abandon a God-given dream. But "they that wait upon the LORD shall renew their strength; they shall mount up with wings as eagles; they shall run, and not be weary" (Isaiah 40:31, KJV).

Prayer gives us the strength and courage to trust God's timing. For it takes *strength* to resist what seems "good" and *courage* to wait for God's best. The psalmist wrote, "Wait patiently for the LORD. Be brave and courageous. Yes, wait patiently for the LORD" (Psalm 27:14). Therefore, pray during this season of waiting, and trust that God's best is worth the wait.

STRENGTH IN THE WORD

There is an appointed time for everything.

ECCLESIASTES 3:1, NASB

TODAY I DECLARE

I'll follow God's timing, not my own.

PRAYERFUL THOUGHTS

Dear Lord,

If it were up to me, I wouldn't wait any longer. I would make this thing happen right now. But your way is the best way, and your timing is right. So I'm yielding to your plan.

Help me to say no, O Lord, to everything that falls outside your will. Give me the strength to endure and the patience to wait. I'm choosing your best, instead of settling for what seems good.

In Jesus' name, amen.

✱ KEEPSAKE

"God's best is worth the wait."

11. Twist of Nature

For Hope beyond the Darkness

Small Green Crested Flycatcher

THE COMMON EVENING PRIMROSE is a beautiful yellow flower that blooms only at night. Through this interesting and ironic twist of nature, God draws our attention to a spiritual lesson: *There is no circumstance so dim—and no darkness so profound—that God can't create beauty in the midst of darkness.*

In Genesis 1:1-2, the Bible teaches, "In the beginning . . . the earth was formless and empty, and darkness covered the deep waters." And similarly, there will be times when the darkness of life attempts to cover our hope. But just as God designed the evening primrose to sprout at night, he created you to blossom beyond the darkness of your sorrows.

Truly remarkable, the evening primrose is more than a pretty flower. It's a medicinal giant that's used to treat a variety of ailments. Though sprung in the dark, it heals, soothes, and rejuvenates. So as you pray through the difficult seasons of your life, let the Lord sustain your hope. He will open your eyes to the good that's blooming.

STRENGTH IN THE WORD

I pray that God, the source of hope, will fill you completely with joy and peace.

ROMANS 15:13

TODAY I DECLARE

I will plant my hope in the Lord.

PRAYERFUL THOUGHTS

Dear Lord,

It would be great if growth sprouted solely from good times. But I know that's not how this life works. Instead, there's a time and divine purpose for everything: "A time to cry and a time to laugh. A time to grieve and a time to dance" (Ecclesiastes 3:4). So I pray for everlasting hope—hope that never wanes. Please show me the beauty that's blooming beyond the night.

In Jesus' name, amen.

KEEPSAKE

"Blossom beyond the darkness of your sorrows."

12. Apply the Filter

For Examining Advice

Yellow Red-poll Warbler

AS LEGEND TELLS IT, two beggars sat on the side of the road. One said, "I'm where I am today because I wouldn't listen to anyone's advice." The other retorted, "I'm where I am today because I took everyone's advice."

Seeking the right counsel is so critical that presidents have cabinets and corporations have boards. It's widely understood that advice is needed. Proverbs 11:14 declares, "In the abundance of [wise and godly] counselors there is victory" (AMP). But not every so-called "godly" message should be heeded.

Prayer is the filter that separates *godly* counsel from the foolish and faulty. This is crucial because even prophets lie! In 1 Kings 13, an old prophet said to a man, "'An angel gave me a message from the Lord.' . . . But the old man was lying" (verse 18, TLB).

Through the purifying systems of Scripture and prayer, God verifies which advice to trust. Through *peace,* you'll receive God's confirmation. Through *unease,* you'll know that the advice was not from God.

▸◂ STRENGTH IN THE WORD

Test everything that is said.

1 THESSALONIANS 5:21

◂▸ TODAY I DECLARE

I'll heed when I feel peace.

PRAYERFUL THOUGHTS

Dear Lord,

I sought advice about this decision, but I still don't know what to do. Some say do *this*; others say do *that*. Where do *you* fall along this spectrum?

Please speak to my spirit, O Lord. Reveal which advice I should take. Do you agree with any of these opinions, or do you have a different idea in mind?

Kindly confirm your thoughts on this decision, as I filter these options through you.

In Jesus' name, amen.

* KEEPSAKE

"God verifies which advice to trust."

13. Added Years

For Restoring Lost Time

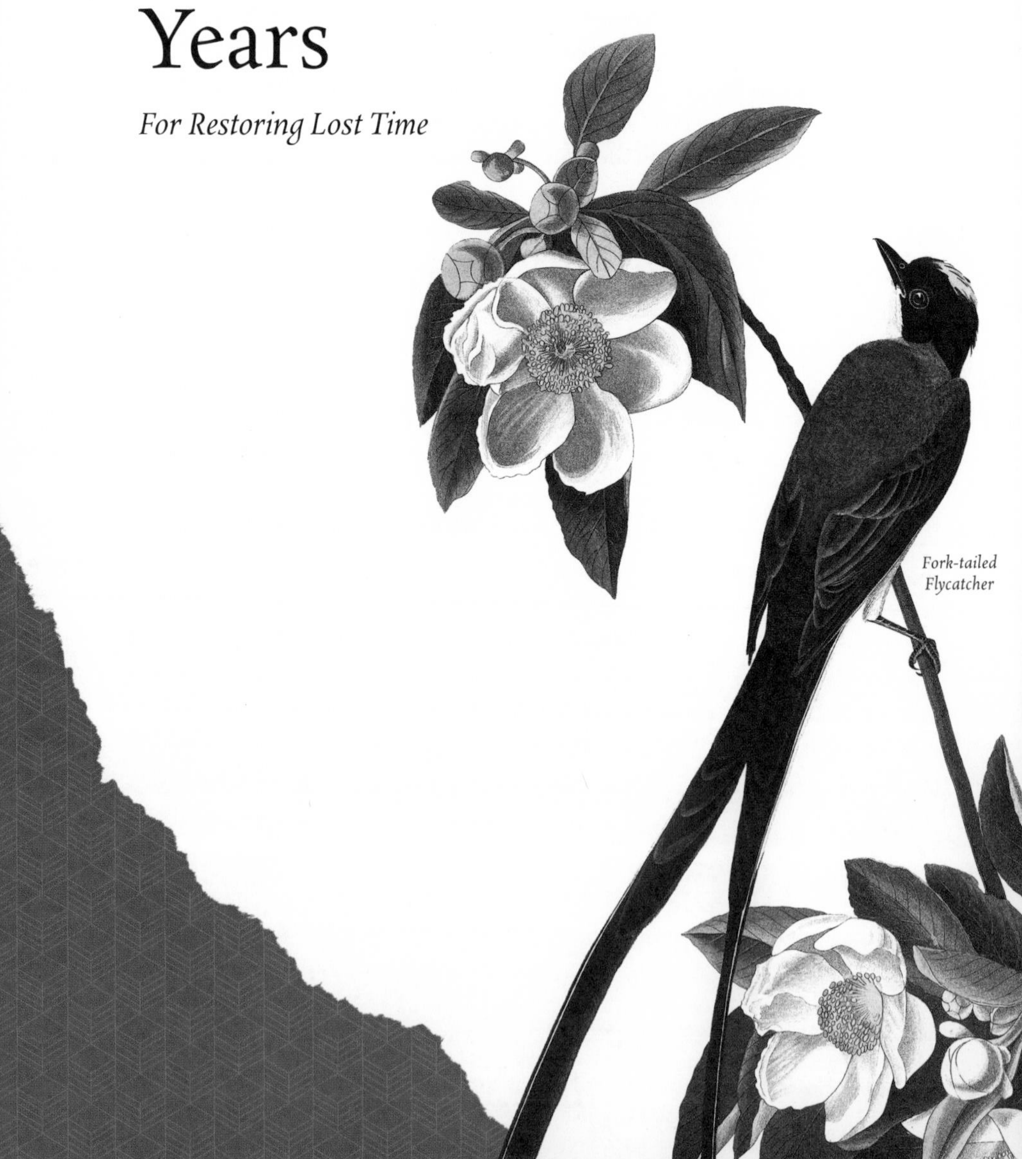

WHEN I WAS YOUNGER, I spent so much time feeling sick, I didn't expect to live long. I told myself that I was biding my time, waiting to meet the Lord. Then, age *fifteen* turned into *twenty*—and *twenty* turned into *twenty-five*. That's when I realized that God wasn't done with me yet.

Maybe you feel like you've wasted too much time—in bad health, in a bad marriage, or simply while being bad. But the Lord has firmly declared, "*I will restore to you the years*" (Joel 2:25, ESV, emphasis added).

In 2 Kings 20, the prophet Isaiah delivered a death sentence to Hezekiah: "The LORD says: Set your affairs in order, for you are going to die." But Hezekiah "turned his face to the wall and prayed." Then God added *fifteen years* to his life (see verses 1-6).

Our God is a years-adding, life-stretching, merciful Father. Like Hezekiah, you can turn your face to the wall and pray, "Lord, lengthen my years."

STRENGTH IN THE WORD

God, your God,
will restore everything.

DEUTERONOMY 30:3, MSG

TODAY I DECLARE

It's not too late.

PRAYERFUL THOUGHTS

Dear Lord,

You held the sun and moon for Joshua, and you lengthened Hezekiah's years. Could you please extend the same mercy and kindness toward me?

I believe that you can do the impossible. I've seen your track record for grace. You've moved the greatest mountains. You've opened the sea. You've healed brokenness, and you've cured disease. So I'm asking you, O Lord: "*Please lengthen my years.*"

In Jesus' name, amen.

KEEPSAKE

"God added fifteen years to his life."

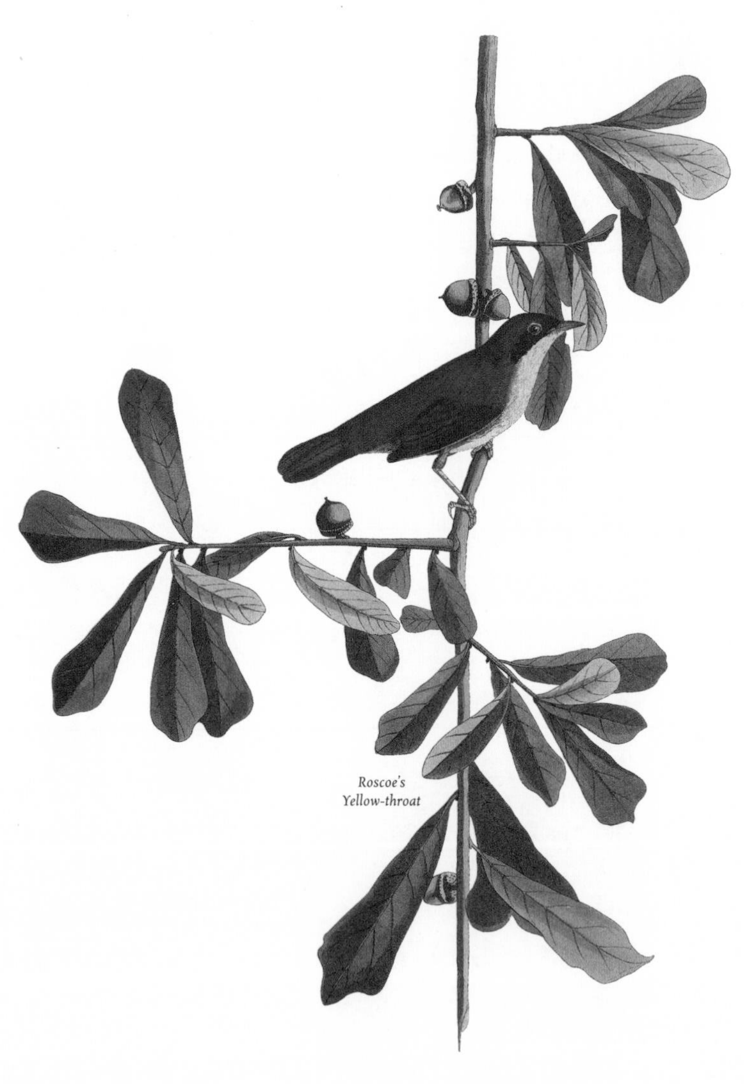

Roscoe's
Yellow-throat

PRAYER SHOULD BE

THE KEY

OF THE DAY

AND THE LOCK

OF THE NIGHT.

GEORGE HERBERT

14. Your Unique Approach

For Exploring Your Ministry

Band-tailed Pigeon

EVERY BELIEVER IS CALLED to spread the gospel. Although we're not all missionaries or Sunday school teachers, we were each created to minister in a unique way. Romans 12:6 teaches, "God has given us different gifts for doing certain things well."

Harriet Powers, born a slave, became a renowned quilt maker. With no formal training, she created Bible-quilt masterpieces, including one that is owned by the Smithsonian National Museum of American History in Washington, D.C.

Harriet used her extraordinary appliqué and piecework techniques to weave biblical scenes. Her woven layers of storytelling include a depiction of the Garden of Eden; Jacob's dream; the Crucifixion; Judas and the thirty pieces of silver; the Last Supper; and many others. In an early twentieth-century article (published by *The Outlook* magazine), Harriet stated that she made her quilts "to preach the Gospel in patchwork."

Similarly, God has called you to share the gospel—possibly in an unconventional way. Harriet ministered through quilts, so maintain an open mind while exploring your unique, God-given approach.

STRENGTH IN THE WORD

[Christ] ordered us to preach everywhere and to testify.

ACTS 10:42

TODAY I DECLARE

I am the Lord's messenger—created to spread his light.

PRAYERFUL THOUGHTS

Dear Lord,

Before I was born, you knew me, and you declared that I would be a light in this world. So, Lord, show me how I'm called to minister—to my family, to my community, and to those who are lost. Please point out my strongest gifts and open my mind to untapped possibilities.

Unveil how I can spread the gospel in a unique and impactful way.

In Jesus' name, amen.

KEEPSAKE

"We were each created to minister."

15. The Battle Is Already Won

For Claiming Victory

Chipping Sparrow

CHRISTIANITY IS ABOUT LOVE AND FORGIVENESS—but it's also about a spiritual war. Satan prowls around like a roaring lion looking for someone to destroy (1 Peter 5:8). The truth is, just as God uses people to *bless* us, the devil uses people to *harm* us. Delilah trapped Samson with her deceit, and Jezebel tormented Elijah by instilling fear. The devil also slyly used Peter. But "Jesus turned to Peter and said, 'Get away from me, Satan! You are a dangerous trap to me'" (Matthew 16:23).

We're in a spiritual battle with an enemy who doesn't fight fair. He'll use your friends, family, coworkers—and yes, even fellow believers. (*Church hurt* is a real and common thing.) But when you pray, God shows up and takes over. Schemers are outwitted, and accusers are silenced. God blocks every harmful plan. Prayer also opens your eyes—so you can look beyond people and target your real enemy. With the Lord by your side, even your toughest battles are already won.

STRENGTH IN THE WORD

He will fight for you
against your enemies, and
he will give you victory!

DEUTERONOMY 20:4

TODAY I DECLARE

I place my battles
in God's hands.

PRAYERFUL THOUGHTS

Dear Lord,

I bring my challenges before you and plead for your help. I'm facing a battle that I can't win on my own. But you, O Lord, are my defender—my undefeated champion and friend. You stand before giants, and they quiver at your strength. Rise up, and display your power. Rise up, and bring the devil to shame.

Hurry, my unconquerable defender. Deliver victory without delay.

In Jesus' name, amen.

KEEPSAKE

"Target your real enemy."

16. Just Because

For Building Friendship

WRITTEN AS A POEM in 1855, "What a Friend We Have in Jesus" has comforted many souls throughout the world. The beloved hymn describes the Lord's never-failing, ever-redeeming friendship; a relationship that's forged through prayer:

What a friend we have in Jesus,
all our sins and griefs to bear.
What a privilege to carry
everything to God in prayer.

As I sing those lyrics, I can't help but wonder, *Does God count us as friends?*

Truth is, God is everyone's friend—but we're not all his friends. In Isaiah 41:8, God classifies his children into three categories: servants, chosen people, and friends. "People of Israel, you are my servants. People of Jacob, I chose you. You are from the family of my friend Abraham" (NCV).

A friend of God prays, even when she doesn't need anything. She dials up, chitchats, and calls his name—just because. By faith, she builds a relationship with a God she can't see; and through her faith, God calls her his friend.

STRENGTH IN THE WORD

Abraham became God's friend.

JAMES 2:23, CEV

TODAY I DECLARE

God is my friend, and
I'm determined to be his.

PRAYERFUL THOUGHTS

Dear Lord,

You've been a good friend to me; far better than I could ever hope. You've stuck closer than any brother; you've loved me through thick and thin.

Now, tell me, O Lord—*how can I be a friend to you*? Like Abraham, who was faithful and obedient, I want my life to bring you joy. Therefore, shape me into a faithful friend—whom you can chat with and trust.

In Jesus' name, amen.

* KEEPSAKE

"A friend of God prays."

17. Tell Me Who I Am

For Silencing Self-Doubt

NETFLIX'S DRAMA *THE CROWN* is one of my favorite shows. If you love period pieces and history, you should definitely watch it! The series chronicles the fascinating reign of Queen Elizabeth II. In one episode, it was revealed that the queen envied Jacqueline Kennedy's grace and beauty. Yes, "Her Majesty the Queen"—with all her riches, titles, and power—envied another woman.

Having moments of envy doesn't make you an awful person; it makes you human. With all the oversharing (and boasting) spewing out in this world, it's easy to feel inadequate. But through prayer, God will silence your self-doubt and tell you who you are:

> *You are the daughter of the Most High King—far more precious than the finest stones. Your ashes have been transformed into beauty, and your uncertainties are nevermore. Your self-esteem is grounded in Jesus, and you are capable and wonderfully made. Your Father is the King of kings and Lord of lords. Oh, yes, that is who you are.*

STRENGTH IN THE WORD

You are altogether beautiful, my darling, beautiful in every way.

SONG OF SOLOMON 4:7

TODAY I DECLARE

I am who God says I am.

PRAYERFUL THOUGHTS

Dear Lord,

I know that it's not right, but I struggle with jealousy. I sometimes look at others and envy what they have. Yet I thank you for allowing me to be honest, and I ask that you remove the envy from my heart.

Set me free, O Lord. Silence the self-doubt that plays in my head, and give me a genuine love for who I am.

In Jesus' name, amen.

* KEEPSAKE

"Your self-esteem is grounded in Jesus."

18. Seize the Opportunity

For Choosing Joy

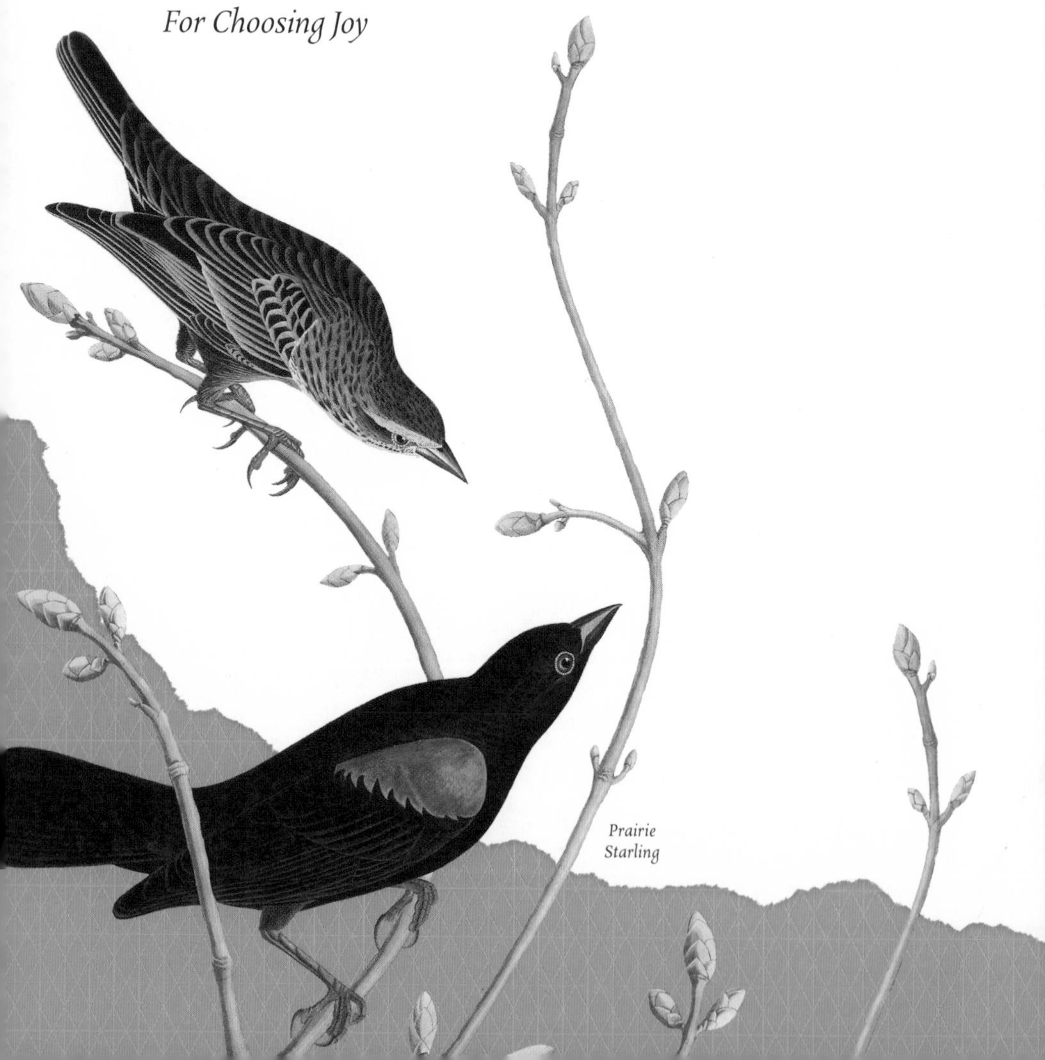

Prairie Starling

I ONCE INTERVIEWED A WOMAN who reminisced joyfully about having her electricity cut off. Although it was a tough financial season, she grew closer to her husband. The couple would have romantic, candlelit, canned-food dinners after their children went to bed. And they learned how to be rich in joy while they were poor in material things. Not surprisingly, this couple didn't stay poor for long. Within five years of their joy-filled poverty, they became millionaires.

Joy is a choice. Unlike happiness, it cannot be stolen when our circumstances change. Joy prays, "I can rejoice because God is with me; I can sleep because the Lord has already carved out a way."

The apostle James wrote, "Dear brothers and sisters, when troubles of any kind come . . . consider it an opportunity for great joy" (James 1:2).

Choosing joy doesn't mean ignoring reality. But in the words of Walt Disney, it means "around here . . . we don't look backwards for very long. We keep moving forward"—with our eyes on what's good.

STRENGTH IN THE WORD

Be joyful in hope, patient in affliction, faithful in prayer.

ROMANS 12:12, NIV

TODAY I DECLARE

Nothing will steal my joy.

PRAYERFUL THOUGHTS

Dear Lord,

I long for the joy that always lasts. Therefore, place me on the path that leads to you. For in your presence, there is fullness of joy, and at your right hand, there are everlasting pleasures. Wherever I am, please remain with me. Wherever you go, don't leave me behind.

During life's highs and lows, every peak and valley, I'll choose joy—because you're with me.

In Jesus' name, amen.

✻ KEEPSAKE

"Be rich in joy."

19. Trust Him

For Financial Provision

IN THE BOOK OF MALACHI, God unveiled the secret to obtaining financial security. What's more, he backed this revelation with a daring promise: "Bring all the tithes into the storehouse so there will be enough food in my Temple. If you do . . . I will open the windows of heaven for you. I will pour out a blessing so great you won't have enough room to take it in! Try it! Put me to the test!" (3:10).

God dares us to *test* him with our financial tithe—but tithing requires faith that may come only through prayer. It takes faith to give 10 percent of *all* your income—come rain or shine. And it takes faith to bring the tithe to God's temple—the actual *church* where you're spiritually fed.

So answer God's dare, and trust him with your tithe. The Lord avows that "your crops will be abundant. . . . Then all nations will call you blessed" (Malachi 3:11-12).

STRENGTH IN THE WORD

One-tenth . . .
belongs to the LORD.

LEVITICUS 27:30

TODAY I DECLARE

I can give anywhere, but my *tithe* belongs to God's church.

PRAYERFUL THOUGHTS

Dear Lord,

Surely, you must know that money is tight, and it's hard to trust the modern-day church. But I'm placing my faith in you, O Lord; not in people nor my scarcity.

Please release the dividends of your biblical promise as I trust you with my financial tithe. Pour out a blessing so great that I won't have enough room to take it all in.

In Jesus' name, amen.

KEEPSAKE

"Giving requires faith that may come only through prayer."

20. The Right Person

For Selecting a Prayer Partner

White-throated Sparrow

THERE IS SUPERNATURAL, UNSTOPPABLE POWER in agreement. In Matthew 18:19 Jesus declared, "If two of you agree here on earth concerning anything you ask, my Father in heaven will do it for you" (Matthew 18:19). This biblical promise doesn't say that God *might* do it—or that he'll *probably* do it. It says that God *will* do it—if we agree.

The Message Bible presses further: "Take this most seriously: A yes on earth is yes in heaven; a no on earth is no in heaven. What you say to one another is eternal. I mean this. When two of you get together on anything at all on earth and make a prayer of it, my Father in heaven goes into action."

That translation is powerful, and it helps explain why the devil sows discord among believers. When we pray together, our prayers are fortified—but partnering with the right person is key. Pick someone whose heart and faith are aligned with yours, and watch God go into action.

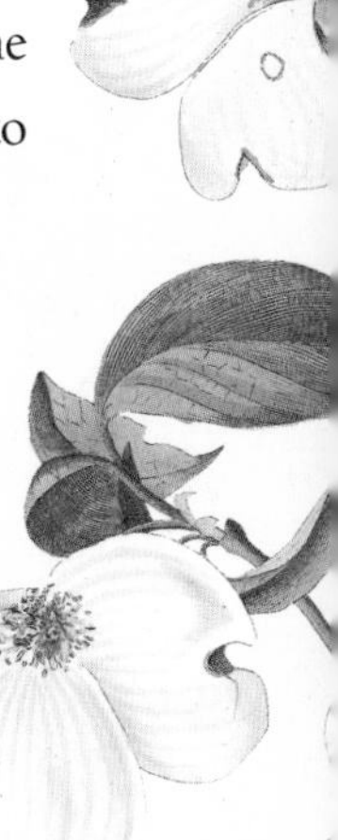

STRENGTH IN THE WORD

Make every effort to keep yourselves united in the Spirit.

EPHESIANS 4:3

TODAY I DECLARE

I will be the kind of prayer partner I hope to have.

PRAYERFUL THOUGHTS

Dear Lord,

Please send me a prayer partner—someone I can trust, and someone who can also trust me. Make it clear who this person is, and allow our hearts to be aligned.

In advance, I come against all sources of jealousy, betrayal, and strife—and I declare harmony over this divinely orchestrated partnership. May your Spirit bring us together, and may our prayers be favored by you.

In Jesus' name, amen.

* KEEPSAKE

"When we pray together, our prayers are fortified."

21. "No"

For Denied Prayers

IN *THEOLOGY OF PRAYER*, author Benjamin Morgan Palmer tells a compelling story of a woman who desperately wanted to see her children. After spending the summer away, she tried to purchase a ticket to sail home. But to her grave disappointment, the ship was fully booked. A few days later, the woman was told shocking news: *The ship never reached its destination.* Instead, it had sunk to the bottom of the Atlantic Ocean.

When we pray, God always weighs our requests against the bigger picture. That explains his no to David (1 Chronicles 17:4), his no to Paul (2 Corinthians 12:8-9), and his no to Jesus in the garden of Gethsemane (Luke 22:42).

The Lord said, "Just as the heavens are higher than the earth, so my ways are higher than your ways and my thoughts higher than your thoughts" (Isaiah 55:9).

Although a negative answer may be tough to appreciate, we must celebrate God's no as much as we celebrate his yes. His answers protect us and reflect the bigger picture.

STRENGTH IN THE WORD

Everything I plan
will come to pass.

ISAIAH 46:10

TODAY I DECLARE

God’s no is a blessing.

PRAYERFUL THOUGHTS

Dear Lord,

I surrender to your answer, for there must be a reason for this decision.

Though I can't see it now or fully understand your ways, I place my trust in your love for me and your plans for the bigger picture.

Please increase my discernment and show me the good in this no. Help me to understand your thoughts and intentions.

In Jesus' name, amen.

* KEEPSAKE

"His answers protect us."

22. They Matter

For the Right Motives

IT'S AMAZING HOW TWO PEOPLE can perform the same action yet get different responses. Like the person who shoves you to shield you from danger, and the person who shoves you to cut into the checkout line.

When we pray, our *motives* matter, and they impact God's response. The story of Hannah teaches that lesson. Every year, Elkanah and his wives traveled to the Tabernacle. "Year after year it was the same—Peninnah would taunt Hannah" (1 Samuel 1:7). This rivalry persisted because Peninnah had children and Hannah had none.

But one day Hannah's motives changed. She no longer hoped for a child to cover her shame and outdo her rival. Instead, she prayed for the opportunity to glorify God: "LORD . . . if you will look upon my sorrow and answer my prayer and give me a son, then I will give him back to you" (1 Samuel 1:11). And the Lord answered Hannah's prayer.

Why we pray matters as much as *what* we pray. God sees—and responds to—the motives of the heart.

STRENGTH IN THE WORD

Put me on trial, LORD, and cross-examine me. Test my motives and my heart.

PSALM 26:2

TODAY I DECLARE

Bad motives will no longer hinder my prayers.

PRAYERFUL THOUGHTS

Dear Lord,

Thank you for being a God who sees everything. Your omniscience holds me accountable; it compels me to do what's right.

Please forgive me for having self-centered and questionable motives. My prayers should be about *you and me*, but they've become more about *only me*. Therefore, redirect my heart to a God-centered place. Let glorifying and pleasing you be the motivating forces behind my prayers.

In Jesus' name, amen.

* KEEPSAKE

"God sees—and responds to—the motives of the heart."

23. Verify

For Testing Emotions

Mangrove Cuckoo

DID YOU KNOW THAT PEPPERS ARE FRUITS? They look like vegetables and are served like vegetables, but they're *not* vegetables. In life, we encounter many things that aren't what they appear to be. That's especially true when it comes to what our emotions tell us.

The fact is, emotions lie. They told Elijah that Jezebel was going to kill him, and they told Sarah that she couldn't conceive. The Israelites were also misguided by their emotions. In Numbers 13, Moses sent twelve men to spy out Canaan—the land that God had promised to give his people. But despite the Lord's vow, ten reported what they *felt*: "[The Canaanites] are stronger than we are! . . . Next to them we felt like grasshoppers" (verses 31 and 33). But Caleb—having seen the *same* land and the *same* giants—gave a different report: "We can certainly conquer [Canaan]!" (verse 30).

Our emotions and reality will often differ, but a "prayer test" reveals which report you should believe. Simply leave your emotions with God in prayer, and give him time to verify the facts.

▸◂ STRENGTH IN THE WORD

Lead me by your truth
and teach me.

PSALM 25:5

◂▸ TODAY I DECLARE

I will wait upon the Lord.
He will reveal the truth.

PRAYERFUL THOUGHTS

Dear Lord,

Thank you for giving me emotions. I can't overlook all the good they produce. They help me love people and feel compassion; they create memories and other wonderful things. But please endow me with a high level of discernment—so I can always know when my feelings are wrong. Help me to verify the facts and veto the lies.

In Jesus' name, amen.

KEEPSAKE

"Leave your emotions with God in prayer."

24. View It Differently

For Benefiting from Rejection

Small Green
Crested Flycatcher

REJECTION CAN BE BOTH PAINFUL AND EMBARRASSING, but there are many interesting things about it. For one, it's universal. At some point in our lives, we'll all feel the sting of rejection. Oddly, the most exclusive journal in the world is called the *Journal of Universal Rejection*. No matter the quality of work, or who submits an article, *everyone* gets rejected.

It's time for us to view rejection differently, because it's a helpful part of the human experience. It thickens our skin, unveils our purpose, and leads us onto the right path. The Bible is full of extraordinary people who were rejected in some form or fashion: Jesus, David, Joseph, Hannah . . . *yet* rejection paved the way to their purpose. First Peter 2:4 states, "[Though Jesus] was rejected by people, . . . he was chosen by God for great honor."

I know that it might not feel this way, but rejection is for your good. Yes, pray for strength to move beyond your pain, but give thanks—because rejection is benefiting you.

STRENGTH IN THE WORD

The LORD has made everything for its purpose.

PROVERBS 16:4, ESV

TODAY I DECLARE

This experience will not crush me.

PRAYERFUL THOUGHTS

Dear Lord,

Because my life is blessed and guided by you, I give thanks for this rejection. Does it feel good? No, *absolutely not*. But somehow I trust that you'll use this experience to benefit me.

Psalm 37:23 encourages, "The LORD directs the steps of the godly. He delights in every detail of their lives." So strengthen my heart and help me move past this pain, while you turn this rejection into a blessing.

In Jesus' name, amen.

* KEEPSAKE

"Rejection is benefiting you."

25. Be Courageous

For Facing Fear

Yellow Red-poll Warbler

YOU'VE PROBABLY HEARD THAT IT'S IMPORTANT to pray against fear—but I'm here to tell you that it's more important to pray for *courage*. History proves that fear may never go away, yet we're called to charge forward despite the angst that we feel. In fact, Jesus carried out his calling even as "sweat fell to the ground like great drops of blood" (Luke 22:44).

The greatest among us don't wait for fear to go away. In 1933, President Franklin D. Roosevelt proclaimed, "The only thing we have to fear is fear itself." Yet, this heroic leader—who led America during a depression and a world war—had an extreme fear of fire. And Moses also dealt with his share of fears. When God told Moses to lead the Israelites out of Egypt, he pleaded, "No, Lord, please send someone else" (Exodus 4:13, GNT).

God has appointed you to answer your calling. And if you're scared, just do it afraid. Pray that courage will overtake you, even if your fears don't go away.

STRENGTH IN THE WORD

Be strong and courageous!

DEUTERONOMY 31:6

TODAY I DECLARE

My faith is stronger than my fears.

PRAYERFUL THOUGHTS

Dear Lord,

I'm afraid, but I'm placing my faith in you. For you're the God who gives assignments, and your assignments come with the necessary strength.

Please fill me with a new endowment of courage—a boldness that overrides my fears. Though I'm fearful, I know that you'll protect me. Though I'm scared, my faith will conquer it all. Like every heroine you called before me, I'll charge forward—in spite of my fear.

In Jesus' name, amen.

✱ KEEPSAKE

"Pray that courage will overtake you."

26. Touch Their Hearts

For Adding Praise

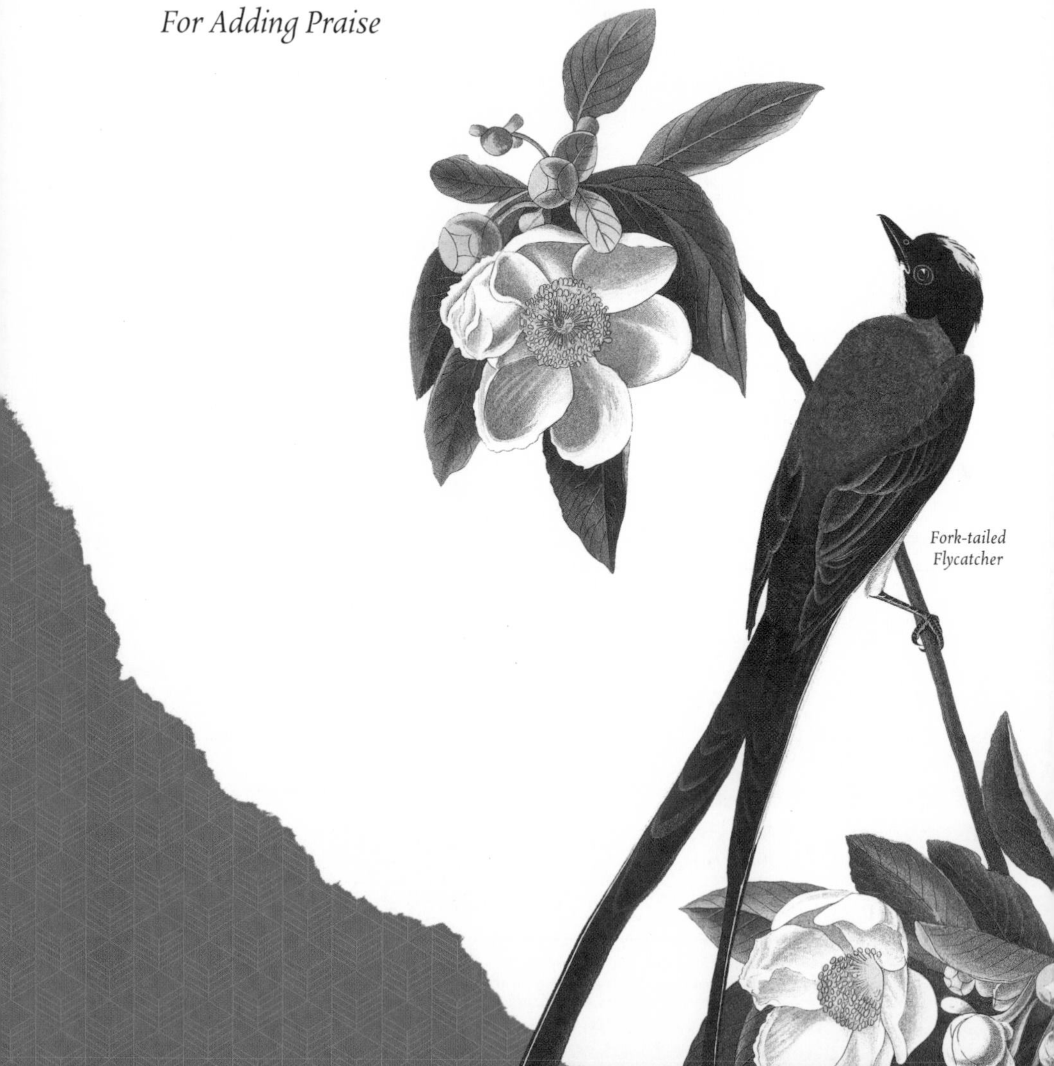

WHEN I CONSIDER THE CONCEPT of praising people, good things don't always come to mind—I think of the terms *sycophants, flatterers, fawners,* and the like. But *genuine* praise has the power to touch hearts and bolster prayers.

People naturally gravitate toward those who uplift them. God himself shows up when we praise his name. Psalm 100:4 invites, "Enter his gates with thanksgiving; go into his courts with praise. Give thanks to him and praise his name." Psalm 22:3 adds that God *inhabits* the praises of his people.

If you've been praying about a challenging family member or friend, try backing your prayers with genuine praise. While in prayer, ask the Lord to help you compile a list of that person's praiseworthy attributes and accomplishments. And be sure to include items that you typically don't mention. When your praise is consistent and genuine, the seeds of your prayers will take deeper roots.

A wise woman once said, "A word of praise can touch a loved one's heart and yield an answer to a stubborn prayer."

STRENGTH IN THE WORD

Encourage one another and build each other up.

1 THESSALONIANS 5:11, NIV

TODAY I DECLARE

I'll be an uplifting voice.

PRAYERFUL THOUGHTS

Dear Lord,

Thank you for choosing me to be a voice of praise in ____________'s life. I'm willing to be whomever you need me to be.

Please fill my mouth with sincere praises that are received by a welcoming ear. And let my efforts take root in ____________'s heart, so ____________ will turn to you.

In Jesus' name, amen.

✱ KEEPSAKE

"Yield an answer to a stubborn prayer."

White-crowned Sparrow

PRAYER IS

PUTTING ONESELF

IN THE HANDS

OF GOD.

MOTHER TERESA

27. Free Yourself

For Embracing Forgiveness

Band-tailed Pigeon

IMAGINE SERVING ALMOST FORTY YEARS on death row for a crime you didn't commit. That's what happened to Ricky Jackson. In 1975, a *supposed* eyewitness to a murder lied, and it took the accuser nearly forty years to tell the truth. But instead of holding on to hatred and resentment, Ricky Jackson chose to embrace forgiveness.

Forgiveness is probably the hardest requirement of Christianity. If you ask most people, they can forgive—*until* a certain point. But the ability to forgive beyond the *until* separates believers from the world. Jesus asked, "If you love only those who love you, why should you get credit for that? Even sinners love those who love them!" (Luke 6:32).

When speaking of his accuser, Ricky Jackson said, "For a lot of years I really hated him. . . . But . . . I desperately want to move forward with my life and the only way I can do that is to forgive."

Forgiveness is how we free ourselves from the emotional weight that has us bound.

STRENGTH IN THE WORD

When you are praying, first forgive anyone you are holding a grudge against.

MARK 11:25

TODAY I DECLARE

I release bitterness and resentment from my heart.

PRAYERFUL THOUGHTS

Dear Lord,

You have the power to turn the hearts of kings (Proverbs 21:1), so please turn my heart toward forgiveness. For too long, I've harbored resentment toward ______________ for what was done. But give me the heart to see ______________ through your eyes, because I can no longer carry the heavy weight of unforgiveness. Replace my bitterness with grace, and transform my scars into love.

In Jesus' name, amen.

KEEPSAKE

"Forgiveness is how we free ourselves."

28. Fail-Proof Method

For Attaining God's Promises

GOD'S WORD IS THE ULTIMATE FAIL-PROOF PRAYER. Why? Because Scripture reflects God's will. First John 5:14 reassures, "We are certain God will hear our prayers when we ask for what pleases him" (CEV).

Praying God's Word (by using Scripture to form our prayers) is like depositing a cashier's check; it comes with special security features. While it's possible for anyone to write a *personal* check, there's no guarantee that it will be paid. But a cashier's check is different. The funds are not only authorized, they're assured. Similarly, when we pray God's Word with faith, we're guaranteed to receive what he has promised. John 15:7 promises, "If you remain in me and my words remain in you, you may ask for anything you want, and it will be granted!"

When we run boldly to the throne of God, we can bank on biblical promises. For example, if we pray for *peace* (John 14:27), *joy* (John 15:11), and *favor* (Deuteronomy 28:13), we can receive *even more than we ask* (Ephesians 3:20).

STRENGTH IN THE WORD

No matter how many promises God has made, they are "Yes" in Christ.

2 CORINTHIANS 1:20, NIV

TODAY I DECLARE

All of God's promises belong to me.

PRAYERFUL THOUGHTS

Dear Lord,

Please do exceedingly abundantly above all that I ask, imagine, and think (Ephesians 3:20). When I pass through turbulent waters, be with me. When I walk through fire, don't let me burn (Isaiah 43:2). I will not fear, for you are with me. You, my God, will give me strength and uphold me with your righteous hand (Isaiah 41:10).

In Jesus' name, amen.

* KEEPSAKE

"We can bank on biblical promises."

29. Don't Let It Fester

For Releasing Guilt

GUILT IS NOT ALWAYS BAD. It can be a moral compass that compels people to repent. Believe it or not, the United States Treasury has an official Conscience Fund. Since 1811, it has helped crooks "atone" for their sins. After stealing or cheating on their taxes, people anonymously mail the government cash, money orders, and cashier's checks—with a confession letter—to clear their guilty consciences.

But when guilt festers, it turns into bad guilt—and bad guilt becomes the devil's tool. He uses it to hold us hostage for sins that God has already forgiven. Satan will tell us that we've made too many mistakes and done the unforgivable because he has a Ph.D. in accusations and lies.

The Bible warns that the devil accuses us before God "day and night" (Revelation 12:10). However, through prayer, we can resist the devil and release our guilt. "As distant as the east is from the west, that is how far [God] has removed our sins from us" (Psalm 103:12, ISV)!

STRENGTH IN THE WORD

Wash me clean from my guilt.
Purify me from my sin.

PSALM 51:2

TODAY I DECLARE

I'm forgiven; I'm redeemed;
I'm no longer guilty.

PRAYERFUL THOUGHTS

Dear Lord,

Your Word promises that if I confess my sins, you are faithful and just to forgive my sins and to cleanse me from all unrighteousness (1 John 1:9).

So here I am, Lord—laying my sins at your feet. Please forgive me, and blot out the stains of my disobedience. Lift the weight of my guilt, and silence the condemning voice of the enemy.

In Jesus' name, amen.

KEEPSAKE

"Resist the devil and release your guilt."

30. Mercy

For Heartfelt Repentance

THE SPIRITUAL LAW OF SOWING AND REAPING is as certain as the law of gravity. Whether or not you believe in Newton's theory, there will be consequences if you jump off the Shanghai Tower.

But—what if I told you that our prayers can override certain consequences? Would you believe you possess the power to change God's mind?

"Obeying GOD's orders to the letter," Jonah declared, "In forty days Nineveh will be smashed." As a result, the king frantically issued a proclamation: "Not one drop of water, not one bite of food. . . . Send up a cry for help to God" (Jonah 3:1-9, MSG).

Now, here's where it gets interesting: "When God saw what they had done and how they had put a stop to their evil ways, *he changed his mind* and did not carry out the destruction he had threatened" (Jonah 3:10, NLT, emphasis added).

God is more interested in our hearts than in rendering punishment. Our seeds of heartfelt repentance can cause the Lord's mercy to take root.

STRENGTH IN THE WORD

Go and sin no more.

JOHN 8:11

TODAY I DECLARE

I'm turning away from my sin.

PRAYERFUL THOUGHTS

Dear Lord,

In the words of Psalm 51:

> Have mercy on me, O God, because of your unfailing love. Because of your great compassion, blot out the stain of my sins. . . . Create in me a clean heart, O God. Renew a loyal spirit within me . . . and make me willing to obey you (verses 1, 10-12).

In Jesus' name, amen.

KEEPSAKE

"Our prayers can override certain consequences."

31. Satisfy Your Hunger

For Spiritual Nourishment

Prairie Starling

WHEN I CATCH MYSELF BEING CRANKY for more than one day, I immediately know that I need to withdraw and spend more time with God. Do you sometimes feel this way? Spiritual hunger and physical hunger share some of the same symptoms, and they can both turn us into women we don't want to be. In fact, *hangry* (the clever blend of hungry and angry) is an actual word!

Being irritable, joyless, and moody are spiritual symptoms. Certainly anyone can experience a bad day. (The car breaks down, the roof leaks, and the kids are out of control.) But when one irritable day spirals into a *series* of irritable days, the cure is withdrawing and spending more time in prayer with God.

Prayer is the mechanism that nourishes our souls. Only God can stop the spiritual pangs that dwell within. Luke 5:16 states, "Jesus often withdrew to the wilderness for prayer." And in our own humanity, we'll *often* have to pull away and do the same.

STRENGTH IN THE WORD

He satisfied their hunger with manna—bread from heaven.

PSALM 105:40

TODAY I DECLARE

I will not ignore my spiritual hunger.

PRAYERFUL THOUGHTS

Dear Lord,

I'm starving for your presence. I've been running on empty for too long. With the demands and responsibilities that try to rule my life, I feel depleted—completely drained. Please help me to escape the busyness that leaves me empty. Fill me with the nourishment that you offer. Pour into my spirit until I overflow, and replenish the peace and strength that I need.

In Jesus' name, amen.

✳ KEEPSAKE

"Prayer is the mechanism that nourishes our souls."

32. It's Okay

For Grappling with Anger

I ONCE ASKED *CALLED* MAGAZINE'S READERS to describe God in one word. Most of the responses were predictable: *awesome, merciful, powerful.* But one was surprising. At first, I stared at the word in shock. I also questioned if it was blasphemous. What did this woman mean by *liable*? It's a word we use to describe someone who must answer for a wrong that's been done. Was it okay to express such anger toward God?

The Bible teaches that it's okay to feel angry, especially when life seems unbearable. I once met a woman who had lost her husband, son, cousin, and father-in-law—all in one day. *Who would blame that poor woman for being enraged?* Even Jonah was furious. "He lost his temper. He yelled at GOD" (Jonah 4:1, MSG).

God invites us to share our real emotions through prayer (while remembering that candor can be communicated with respect). Moreover, prayer isn't only for "happy" moments; so pray out the anger that you feel.

STRENGTH IN THE WORD

"Don't sin by letting anger control you." Don't let the sun go down while you are still angry.

EPHESIANS 4:26

TODAY I DECLARE

God has a plan for what I'm going through.

PRAYERFUL THOUGHTS

Dear Lord,

How could you allow this to happen? Surely you knew that it would cause me great pain. Where was your mercy when I needed it? Where was your renowned and unfailing grace? Lord, I want to lean on you and trust in you—but I feel crushed, forgotten, and betrayed.

Please forgive me for my raw tone, and replace my anger with greater faith.

In Jesus' name, amen.

KEEPSAKE

"God invites us to share our real emotions."

33. One Body

For Uplifting Political Leaders

White-throated Sparrow

WHAT WOULD YOU DO if the president of the United States showed up for prayer? Would you welcome him (or her), or would you pray *grudgingly*? One day, the president paid a surprise visit to a church in Virginia, and some members didn't want him there. Ironically, it was a day set aside to pray for the president.

In the Kingdom of God, there is no distinction between Democrats and Republicans, liberals and conservatives. There's *one* body—focused on *one* Kingdom agenda. In fact, the Bible teaches that a nation's strength is rooted in the united prayers of the righteous. The Lord said, "If my people who are called by my name will humble themselves and pray and seek my face and turn from their wicked ways, I will hear from heaven . . . and restore their land" (2 Chronicles 7:14).

As one body, we must offer the sacrifice of wholehearted prayer—even when our political leaders seem undeserving. "Ask God to help them; intercede on their behalf, and give thanks for them" (1 Timothy 2:1).

STRENGTH IN THE WORD

Pray this way for kings
and all who are in authority.

1 TIMOTHY 2:2

TODAY I DECLARE

Praying for our leaders
is my honor and duty.

PRAYERFUL THOUGHTS

Dear Lord,

I can't promise to agree with every political leader—but with a genuine and loving heart, I'll cover them in prayer. Please give our commander in chief the wisdom to make the right decisions—and shield our leader's health and family. Also, guide our legislature, keep our nation safe, and shape the decisions in our courts. May true justice always prevail, and may we faithfully place our trust in you.

In Jesus' name, amen.

KEEPSAKE

"Offer the sacrifice of wholehearted prayer."

34. Learn to Wrestle

For Tenacity

IF I HAD TO PICK A FAVORITE BIBLE CHARACTER, Jacob would be in my top three. He was a man who wrestled for what he desired. Jacob wrestled with Esau for a birthright, wrestled with Laban for a wife, and wrestled with God for a blessing. Jacob told the angel of the Lord, "I will not let you go unless you bless me" (Genesis 32:26).

Some prayers will be answered quickly, but others will require that you put up a fight. Yes, you might have to roll up your prayer-warrior sleeves and wrestle for your breakthrough. That's why Jesus taught his disciples to persist: "One day Jesus told his disciples a story to show that they should always pray and never give up. . . . 'So don't you think God will surely give justice to his chosen people who cry out to him day and night?'" (Luke 18:1, 7).

Therefore, hold on to God like Jacob did, and refuse to let go. The Lord applauds our tenacious prayers.

STRENGTH IN THE WORD

She came and worshiped him, pleading again, "Lord, help me!"

MATTHEW 15:25

TODAY I DECLARE

I won't stop praying and believing for this breakthrough.

PRAYERFUL THOUGHTS

Dear Lord,

I bring this matter before you. Again I'm pleading for your favorable response. Like Jacob, I'm willing to wrestle; like the desperate woman in Matthew 15, I won't give up. Please use this tussle to develop my tenacity, and show me how to pray until a breakthrough is released. But if the request is outside your will, O Lord, quickly remove this desire from my heart.

In Jesus' name, amen.

* KEEPSAKE

"Roll up your prayer-warrior sleeves."

35. Seek the Lord

For Considering Adoption

BY THE TIME THIS BOOK IS RELEASED, I'll be forty years old. That is, forty, never married, and without kids. There's a panic button that goes off when a woman hits a certain age, and it rings louder when she's not yet a mom. But God has been so good, because I've always had this peaceful certainty: *A woman doesn't have to give birth to be a mother.*

Adoption is both a gift and a ministry. It also requires considerable prayer. Inviting God into the process will help you discern whether adopting is the right choice. Plus, it will keep you strong and reveal subconscious motives.

Ephesians 1:5 is a beautiful reminder of God's decision to adopt us: "God decided in advance to adopt us into his own family by bringing us to himself through Jesus Christ. This is what he wanted to do, and it gave him great pleasure."

So seek the Lord, my sister, if you're longing to be an adoptive mom. Follow your heart, and bring along wisdom.

STRENGTH IN THE WORD

Anyone who welcomes a little child like this on my behalf is welcoming me.

MATTHEW 18:5

TODAY I DECLARE

The Lord will give me the desires of my heart.

PRAYERFUL THOUGHTS

Dear Lord,

Like Sarah, Rachel, and Hannah—and *many* other sisters of the faith—I long to be a mother. If it's your will, O Lord, please open the door to adoption, and give me divine favor with everyone involved.

May your Spirit handpick my precious child, and anoint me to be his or her mother.

In Jesus' name, amen.

✻ KEEPSAKE

"Follow your heart, and bring along wisdom."

36. Keep Watch

For Controlling Your Thoughts

Mangrove Cuckoo

DID YOU KNOW THAT NEARLY HALF OF U.S. DOCTORS—and almost all U.K. physicians—prescribe fake meds? Though the ethics are questionable, placebos help many patients feel better. The mere *thought* of treatment can relieve pain, insomnia, and nausea. Our thoughts are that powerful! That's why Proverbs 4:23 forewarns, "Be careful what you think, because your thoughts run your life" (NCV).

Prayer is an effective way to control our thoughts. As prayer warriors, we're not passive bystanders who let in whatever comes our way. Instead, we're spiritual gatekeepers who are commissioned to keep watch over what we think. When Jesus was in the wilderness, Satan tried to tempt him with ungodly ideas. But each time, Jesus resisted (Matthew 4:1-11).

In our prayer lives, we have the authority to accept, reject, welcome, or rebuke every thought—and hold it captive (2 Corinthians 10:5). This is important because our thoughts define who we are (Proverbs 23:7, NASB). Therefore, my sister, carefully keep watch over what enters (and remains) in your mind.

STRENGTH IN THE WORD

May all my thoughts
be pleasing to him.

PSALM 104:34

TODAY I DECLARE

I take control and authority
over my mind.

PRAYERFUL THOUGHTS

Dear Lord,

I take hold of the authority you've given me, and I reject every ungodly idea. I rebuke the hidden thoughts of sin and negativity, and I reject the thoughts of insecurity and self-doubt. Please fix my imagination on what's "true, and honorable, and right, and pure, and lovely" (Philippians 4:8). Renew my mind and help me meditate on more admirable things.

In Jesus' name, amen.

* KEEPSAKE

"Our thoughts define who we are."

37. Power of Influence

For Saying the Right Words

Small Green Crested Flycatcher

SINCE THE BEGINNING OF TIME, women have possessed the power to save and destroy; build up and tear down; start wars and facilitate peace. We accomplished some of these mighty feats through the sheer influence of our words.

This isn't go-girl *feminist talk*; it's go-girl *Bible talk*. The Word of God teaches that a woman's words have power. Wasn't it Delilah's tongue that ruined Samson, and Abigail's words that spared Nabal from David's sword? "Thank God for your good sense!" David said to Abigail. "I have heard what you said" (1 Samuel 25:33, 35).

God has given women the power of influence—which is yet another reason to pray. "A word out of your mouth may seem of no account, but it can accomplish nearly anything. . . . By our speech we can ruin the world, [and] turn harmony to chaos" (James 3:5-6, MSG). With that level of influence, we would be remiss not to pray for the right words to say.

STRENGTH IN THE WORD

Let your speech always be gracious, seasoned with salt.

COLOSSIANS 4:6, ESV

TODAY I DECLARE

I will prayerfully wield my influence.

PRAYERFUL THOUGHTS

Dear Lord,

Thank you for making me a woman of influence. I humbly accept the responsibility that comes with that power.

Please anchor my tongue with the weight of grace and compassion; and may my words be like sweet honey that comforts souls. Help me touch lives with the right words, at the right time, and with the right tone. Guide everything that I say, O Lord.

In Jesus' name, amen.

* KEEPSAKE

"A woman's words have power."

38. New Environment

For a Fresh Start

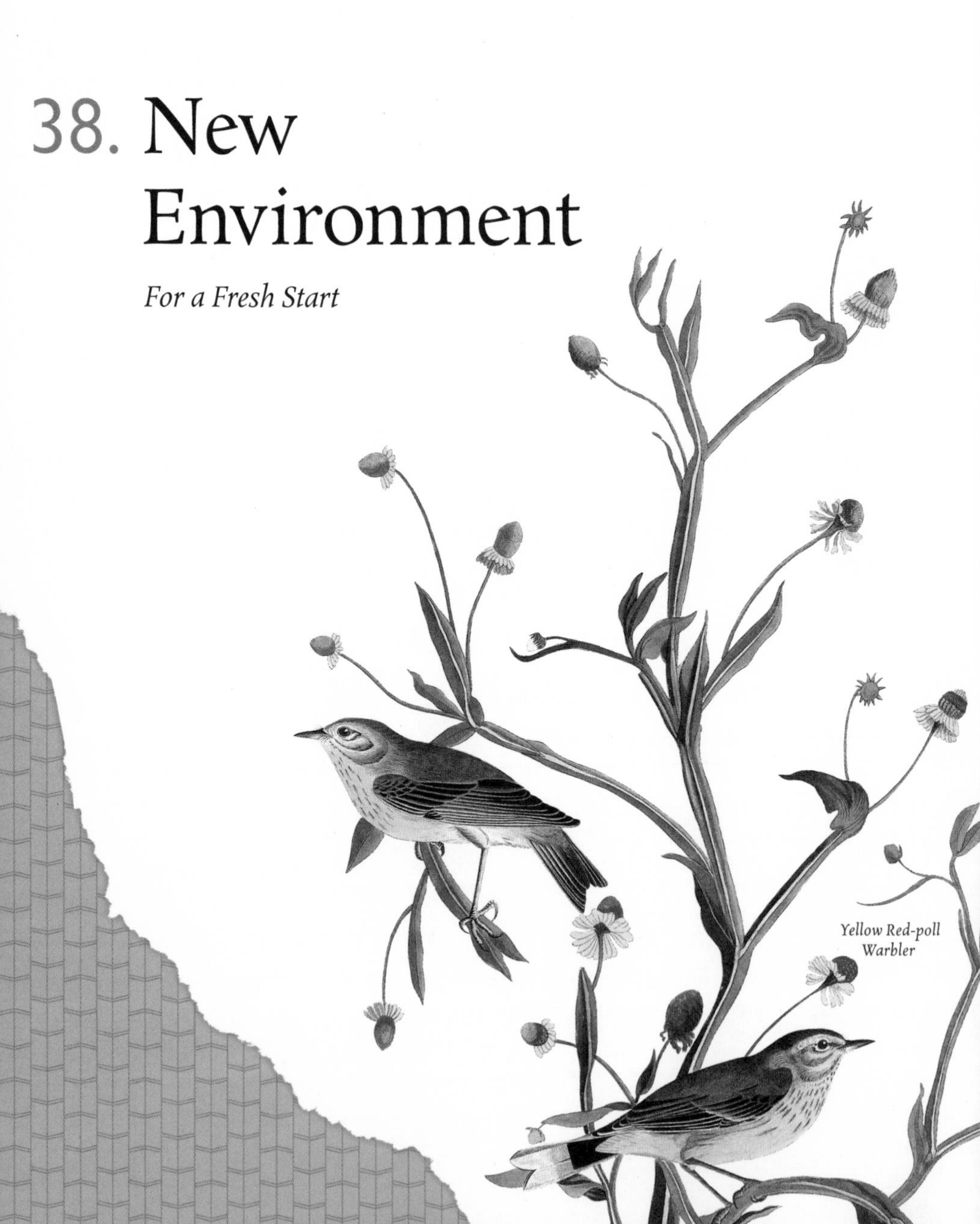

AS A FIRST-GENERATION native-born American, I understand the impact of new environments. Every day, all over the world, migrants rise above feeling stuck. They dare to replant themselves in environments where they can grow. Similarly, sometimes we'll need to be replanted—in a new job, in a new church, or even in a new city.

The Bible teaches that we don't have to live in the "land of stuck." Indeed, we have the power to reposition ourselves. Jesus himself couldn't perform miracles in his hometown—because folks couldn't get over his past. Mark 6:3-6 states, "They scoffed, 'He's just a carpenter' . . . and refused to believe in him. . . . Because of their unbelief, he couldn't do any miracles among them except to place his hands on a few sick people and heal them. . . . He was amazed at their unbelief."

We, too, may be amazed by how an environment limits our potential. But we can pray to be replanted—in a place where we can grow and become all that we were created to be.

STRENGTH IN THE WORD

The old life is gone;
a new life has begun!

2 CORINTHIANS 5:17

TODAY I DECLARE

If I can't grow where I am,
I'll change where I am.

PRAYERFUL THOUGHTS

Dear Lord,

If it's your will, please plant me in a new environment—it's difficult to flourish where I am. Each time I try to move forward, something (or someone) holds me back.

In the words of Jeremiah 17:8, make me "like [a tree] planted along a riverbank"—in an environment where I can sprout, grow, and thrive. Surround me with people who believe in me, and help me get unstuck.

In Jesus' name, amen.

* KEEPSAKE

"We don't have to live in the 'land of stuck.'"

39. Conduct an Analysis

For Growing beyond Failure

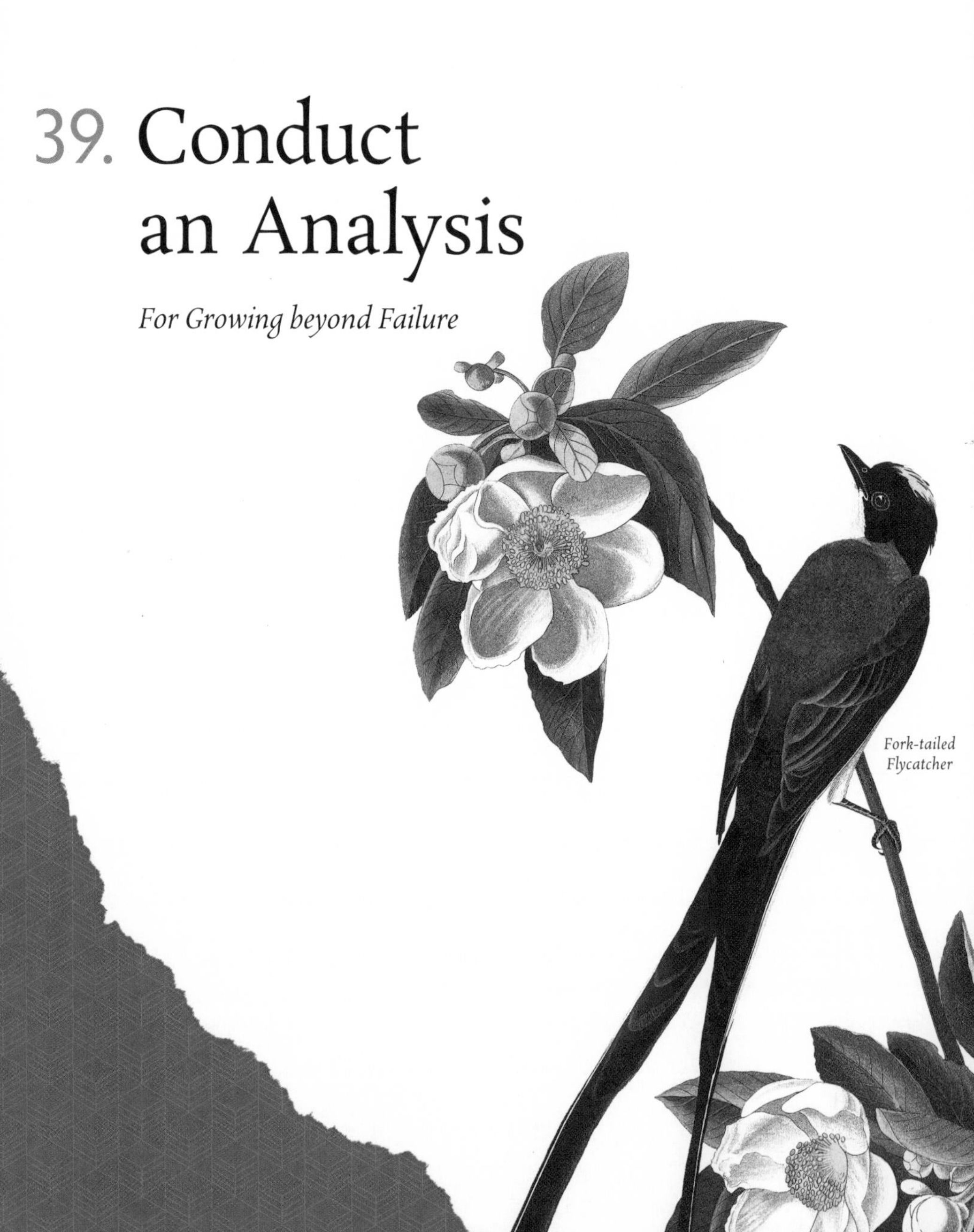

FAILURE IS A VITAL PART OF SUCCESSFUL ENGINEERING. The sinking of the *Titanic*, the collapse of the Tacoma Narrows Bridge, the crumbling of the World Trade Center—each of these catastrophes taught engineers how to avoid future mistakes.

It's called a failure analysis—the process of studying why a failure occurred and how to avoid it in the future. It's hard to overlook the spiritual similarities. Proverbs 24:16 teaches, "The godly may trip seven times, but they will get up again." However, ignoring, blame shifting, or tripping over the *same* mistake is plain foolishness.

Similar to the world of engineering, the Kingdom of God requires that we analyze and learn from our failures. Turning a blind eye (because of shame and denial) leads only to future catastrophes. The sinking of the *Titanic* prompted lifesaving regulations, and our failures can lead to stronger boundaries, healthier relationships, and wiser decisions. Failure is a growth opportunity—and a critical part of future success.

STRENGTH IN THE WORD

Don't turn your back on wisdom, for she will protect you.

PROVERBS 4:6

TODAY I DECLARE

I'm not afraid to grow.

PRAYERFUL THOUGHTS

Dear Lord,

Help me to celebrate the lessons that come from failure, and give me the strength to grow beyond the disappointment and shame.

Focus my heart on gained experience and acquired wisdom, because without them, there can be no growth.

In Jesus' name, amen.

KEEPSAKE

"Failure is a growth opportunity."

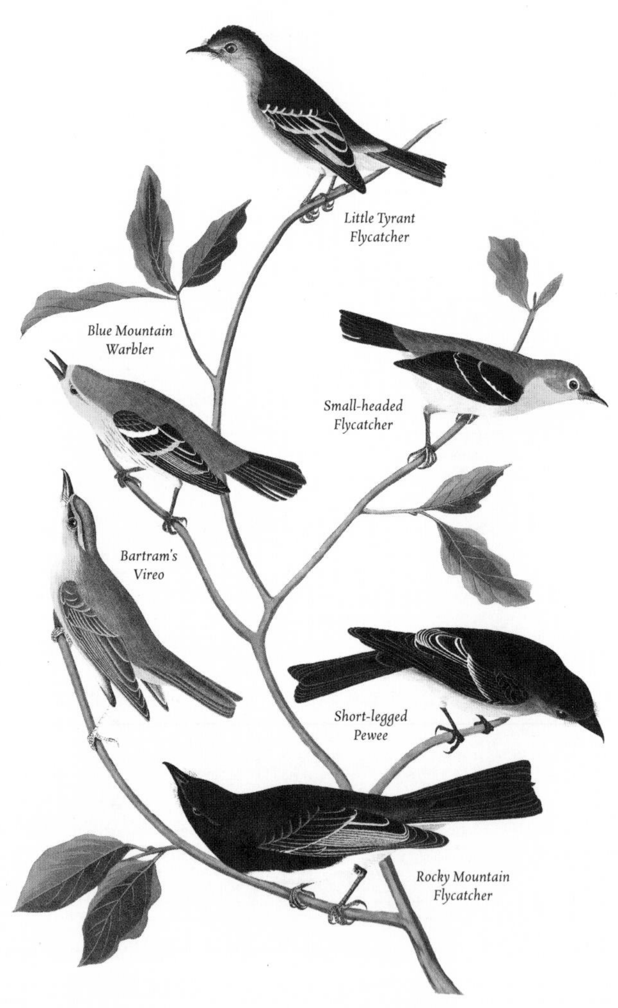
Little Tyrant
Flycatcher
Blue Mountain
Warbler
Small-headed
Flycatcher
Bartram's
Vireo
Short-legged
Pewee
Rocky Mountain
Flycatcher

PRAY HARDEST

WHEN IT'S HARDEST

TO PRAY.

CHARLES H. BRENT

40. Focus on Jesus

For Distractions

Band-tailed Pigeon

IF YOU WERE TO LIST THE DISTRACTIONS in your life, the lineup would probably include things like *social media, text messages, emails,* and *phone calls.* But a distraction is anything that takes our eyes off Jesus. So an accurate list would also include *worry, fear,* and *strife.*

Remarkably, the average person spends more than five years of their life worrying, according to a study conducted by the health-care provider Benenden Health. That means worrying is a *serious* distraction. But God told Moses, "Speak to the People of Israel. Tell them [not to] get distracted by everything you feel or see" (Numbers 15:39, MSG).

In 1868, the French artist Gustave Doré painted a beautiful depiction of Daniel in the lions' den. The painting shows the prophet looking up—focused on God—while surrounded by lions. Throughout our lives, we'll similarly be encircled by circumstances that threaten to turn our gaze away from the Lord; but pray for the strength to "keep your eyes straight ahead; ignore all sideshow distractions" (Proverbs 4:25, MSG).

STRENGTH IN THE WORD

I will . . . fix my eyes on your ways.

PSALM 119:15, ESV

TODAY I DECLARE

The Lord deserves my attention.

PRAYERFUL THOUGHTS

Dear Lord,

If life were about doing things *my* way, I would ask that every distraction be removed. But everything—from my phone to my mood—is a potential distraction. So whatever adjustment needs to happen, please make that change within me.

Redirect my gaze, O Lord, and help me to look straight ahead. Fix my eyes on you—the God who is above all things.

In Jesus' name, amen.

KEEPSAKE

"Worrying is a serious distraction."

41. Benefit All

For Loving Difficult People

Chipping Sparrow

TOXIC PEOPLE. It's a phrase that we use to describe difficult folks. For seemingly valid reasons, we cut them off, ignore them, and block them. Some faith leaders even recommend walking away from these draining, crazy, joy-sucking drama magnets.

Truth be told, this perspective doesn't line up with God's Word; it lines up with our flesh (the part of us that's fed up, exhausted, and annoyed). But Jesus said, "Healthy people don't need a doctor—sick people do" (Mark 2:17).

Telling ourselves *I'll pray for them at a distance* is how we make peace with our "fleshy side." However, unless someone poses a *real* danger to us, we're called to pray not only *for* them, but also *with* them. After all, we're the hands and feet of Christ.

Galatians 6:9 urges, "Let's not allow ourselves to get fatigued doing good. At the right time we will harvest a good crop if we don't give up, or quit. . . . Let us work for the benefit of all" (MSG).

▸◂ STRENGTH IN THE WORD

Pray for all people. Ask God to help them; intercede on their behalf.

1 TIMOTHY 2:1

◂▸ TODAY I DECLARE

I'm the hands and feet of Christ.

PRAYERFUL THOUGHTS

Dear Lord,

At times, I dread interacting with certain people. To be honest, they zap my joy with their negative energy. But you've called your people to reach the brokenhearted and hurting; you've called us to be your hands of compassion and your feet that bring Good News. So please give me the strength to be more like you. Give me a heart that earnestly loves and joyfully serves all people.

In Jesus' name, amen.

KEEPSAKE

"Pray not only for them, but also with them."

42. Joyful or Prickly

For an Attitude Adjustment

AS THE STORY GOES, while former U.S. President Bill Clinton was in Japan, the Japanese prime minister intended to ask him, "How are you?" But instead he accidentally asked, "Who are you?" In response, President Clinton quipped, "I'm Mrs. Clinton's husband."

Each day, the world asks us the same question. On good days, we're often Ms. Joyful. However, on bad days, we tend to become Ms. Prickly.

The Bible teaches that our attitudes are like uniforms. They inadvertently disclose who we are. Police officers' attire tells the world they have authority, and doctors' coats announce they've earned professional respect. So what do *our* attitudes reveal about us?

If you're anything like me, praying for a more godly temperament is a *daily* task. (Crazy drivers alone require that I pray without ceasing.) But the Bible teaches that an attitude adjustment must be taken seriously. It's a "must pray" for every believer. Colossians 3:14 instructs, "Dress in the wardrobe God picked out for you: compassion, kindness, humility, quiet strength, discipline. Be even-tempered" (MSG).

STRENGTH IN THE WORD

Do everything readily and cheerfully.

PHILIPPIANS 2:14, MSG

TODAY I DECLARE

My attitude will represent Christ.

PRAYERFUL THOUGHTS

Dear Lord,

Please forgive me for the many times when I've had a bad attitude.

I'm ashamed to say that my "spiritual attire" doesn't always represent you.

I ask that you temper my ways and help me radiate joy. Please give me an attitude adjustment.

In Jesus' name, amen.

KEEPSAKE

"Our attitudes . . . disclose who we are."

43. Believe Again

For Restoring Hope

DURING WORLD WAR II, an unknown Jew, hiding from the Nazis in Germany, scratched this hope-filled prayer into the wall of a cellar:

I believe in the sun even when it is not shining.
I believe in love even when feeling it not.
I believe in God even when He is silent.

In the midst of the horrors of the Holocaust, this person chose to believe in God and the beauty that life had to offer. He or she was determined to hold on to hope.

If your life experiences have changed the way you see God and life in general, you can believe again. Your prayers can speak hope back into hopelessness and declare the restoration of spiritual light. Even in your darkest hour, you can believe.

Deeply distressed, the prophet Jeremiah chose hope: "GOD's loyal love couldn't have run out, his merciful love couldn't have dried up. They're created new every morning. . . . I'm sticking with God. (I say it over and over.)" (Lamentations 3:22-24, MSG).

STRENGTH IN THE WORD

I still have hope.

RUTH 1:12, NCV

TODAY I DECLARE

I will rise above this sorrow.

PRAYERFUL THOUGHTS

Dear Lord,

When will my sorrows be lifted? It feels like I'm carrying the weight of the world. It's hard to see hope when sorrow fills my eyes, but I still believe in you.

Please lift me out of this depression. If it lasts longer, I may not be able to cope. Help me see light at the end of this road.

Lord, I'll always believe in you.

In Jesus' name, amen.

* KEEPSAKE

"Speak hope back into hopelessness."

44. Be Intentional

For Expressing Gratitude

ACCORDING TO A STUDY conducted on five different continents, people rarely say "thank you." English speakers are somewhat better than others—but on average, we express thanks only 14.5 percent of the time.

"Thank you" is a vital part of any relationship, including our relationship with God. It tells the Lord that he's more than a vending machine that we run to when we need something to eat.

Jesus felt very strongly about intentional gratitude. As he entered a village, ten men with leprosy asked for mercy, and Jesus healed them. But *only one* came back to express gratitude. "He fell to the ground at Jesus' feet, thanking him for what he had done. . . . Jesus asked, 'Didn't I heal ten men? Where are the other nine?'" (Luke 17:16-17).

When we pray, God wants us to *thank* him as much as we *ask* him. A heartfelt thank-you requires an intentional investment of effort. It tells God that he's not someone we use; he's someone we love.

STRENGTH IN THE WORD

I pray that you will be grateful to God.

COLOSSIANS 1:12, CEV

TODAY I DECLARE

I will intentionally express my gratitude.

PRAYERFUL THOUGHTS

Dear Lord,

Thank you for being Jehovah-Jireh, the God who provides; and thank you for being my genuine friend. When I think of all that you've done for me, there are too many blessings to count. You made a way when there was no way; you opened windows when every door was locked.

Thank you for your abounding generosity. I'm grateful for who you are.

In Jesus' name, amen.

KEEPSAKE

"'Thank you' is a vital part of any relationship."

45. Cherish It

For Appreciating Small Beginnings

WE ALL KNOW SUCCESS STORIES, but we don't always know the journey. Like the megaminister who used to sleep in her car because she couldn't afford a hotel room when traveling—or the billionaire entrepreneur who used to walk door-to-door, begging people to buy her products. These are real-life, hard-knock success stories about people who started small.

Zechariah 4:10 encourages, "Do not despise these small beginnings, for the LORD rejoices to see the work begin." God rejoices because first steps are meaningful. For one, they cultivate creativity. The founders of the hospitality giant Airbnb raised start-up capital by selling cereal boxes. (It's true! Look up Obama O's and Cap'n McCain's.)

God uses small starts to develop us in ways that big beginnings can't. When you feel small and insignificant, *pray*—and you'll be reminded that this season is ordained and has purpose. When your spirit is down and depleted, *pray*—and you'll find that God's strength is more than enough.

STRENGTH IN THE WORD

If you are faithful in little things, you will be faithful in large ones.

LUKE 16:10

TODAY I DECLARE

Great things start small.

PRAYERFUL THOUGHTS

Dear Lord,

Small beginnings are discouraging and difficult. At times I wonder, *Is this venture ordained by you? Is it even a good idea?* With not enough support and little progress, I'm not sure I want to go on. Lord, fill me with strength and send creative solutions. Please help this venture grow. You are the God who turns nothings into somethings. So turn my small start into a success story.

In Jesus' name, amen.

KEEPSAKE

"This season is ordained and has purpose."

46. Due upon Receipt

For Reinforcing Boundaries

White-throated Sparrow

WHEN I STARTED *CALLED* MAGAZINE, I knew little about industry standards. So imagine my surprise when I learned that advertisers paid thirty to sixty days *after* signing a contract. It seemed unjust! How could a fledgling company survive with those standards? Consequently, I prayed. And with a dose of chutzpah, backed by necessity, I established a new boundary: "All invoices are due upon receipt."

Boundaries don't just happen. They are prayerfully created. In Exodus 19, the Lord instructed Moses to set boundaries around Mount Sinai to keep animals and people from climbing the mountain. But God commanded one more step: "Go back down and warn the people not to break through the boundaries . . . or they will die. Even the priests who regularly come near . . . must purify themselves" (verses 21-22).

This passage teaches that boundaries must be prayerfully *established* and prayerfully *reinforced*. The two must go hand in hand. We must tell people what boundaries we've created, and then ensure that they don't cross them.

STRENGTH IN THE WORD

I want you to put your foot down.

TITUS 3:8, MSG

TODAY I DECLARE

Boundaries keep me safe.

PRAYERFUL THOUGHTS

Dear Lord,

Please place a hedge of protection around me. Shield me from exploitation and abuse. You know my weaknesses and vulnerabilities; you know which people take advantage of me.

But you, O Lord, are my gallant protector; you, O Lord, are my shield and strength. Please reveal which boundaries I should establish, and give me the courage to maintain them.

In Jesus' name, amen.

✱ KEEPSAKE

"We must tell people what boundaries we've created."

47. Rest & Invest

For Self-Love

AT THE HEART OF WHAT PHILOSOPHER KATE MANNE CALLS the human giver syndrome is the belief that we should value others more than we value ourselves. This belief isn't just false; it's also unbiblical. Mark 12:31 states, "Love others as well as you love yourself" (MSG). "As well as" means equally, and with the same level of quality.

In the Kingdom of God, there's no condemnation for self-love. "On the seventh day God had finished his work of creation, so he rested from all his work" (Genesis 2:2). I know what you're thinking: *God rested because he was done with his work. But, girl, I'm not done with my work!*

Fair enough. However, God rested to establish the importance of caring for ourselves. Besides, there will never be a time when our work is complete. There's always *another* project, *another* obligation, and *another* reason to put ourselves last.

If we struggled with loving someone else, wouldn't we pray for the ability to see them differently? So maybe it's time to pray for the willingness to love *ourselves* more.

STRENGTH IN THE WORD

God will help her.

PSALM 46:5, NASB

TODAY I DECLARE

I deserve love.

PRAYERFUL THOUGHTS

Dear Lord,

Teach me how to love myself. I'm not sure how to accomplish that. I know how to love others, and how to attend to their needs, but I struggle with loving myself.

Please give me a new awakening; a discovery of all that I enjoy and cherish. I'm ready to care for myself as much as I care for others. Please show me the meaning of self-love.

In Jesus' name, amen.

* KEEPSAKE

"There's no condemnation for self-love."

48. Survival Instincts

For Life after Church Hurt

Warbling Flycatcher

IF YOU'RE BEING CHASED BY A BEAR, what do you do? *You run.*

If a meteorite is falling out of the sky, what do you do? *You run.*

Yet for some reason, our survival instincts often check out when it comes to protecting ourselves at church. It's sad how many of our sisters have suffered abuse at the hands of a spiritual leader.

If there's ever a time to pray, it is when deciding if, when, and how to leave one's church. God should be a part of that decision! "This is a trustworthy saying," says the apostle Paul. "'If someone aspires to be a church leader, [they desire] an honorable position.' So a church leader must be a [person] whose life is above reproach, . . . must exercise self-control, live wisely, and have a good reputation" (1 Timothy 3:1-2).

If you discern that it may be time to run, then it's also time to pray. Ask God to send godly support, direction, and clarity.

STRENGTH IN THE WORD

I will guide you along the best pathway for your life.

PSALM 32:8

TODAY I DECLARE

If needed, I will run.

PRAYERFUL THOUGHTS

Dear Lord,

I no longer feel comfortable at my church, but my life isn't based on how I feel. It's predicated on your will and my safety. Therefore, tell me what to do.

Please send someone who has sense and authority; someone who can effectively advocate on my behalf. I can't face this issue on my own.

I need support and guidance.

In Jesus' name, amen.

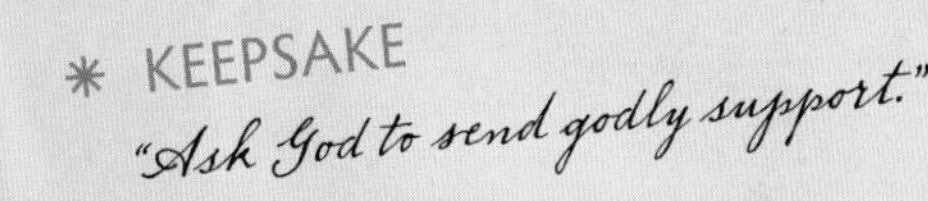
* KEEPSAKE
"Ask God to send godly support."

49. Action Is Required

For Ending Excuses

ITZHAK PERLMAN FELL IN LOVE WITH THE VIOLIN at the age of three. He was determined to become a world-renowned musician. But a year later, he was diagnosed with polio, a disease that crippled his mobility. Many would have given up, but Perlman pressed on. Today, he is celebrated as one of the greatest classical violinists in the world—sometimes performing from his scooter.

In God's Kingdom, there are no excuses. We have to do our part because prayer works with corresponding action. For example, if a debt needs to be paid off, someone must work; and if you want to fulfill a dream, you must take the necessary steps.

Scripture declares, "Faith by itself isn't enough" (James 2:17). *The Message* Bible makes the same point, but with less sugarcoating: "Isn't it obvious that God-talk without God-acts is outrageous nonsense?"

Itzhak Perlman didn't allow polio to be an excuse; he took action! And similarly, when we back our prayers with action, great things will follow.

STRENGTH IN THE WORD

Be doers of the word.

JAMES 1:22, ESV

TODAY I DECLARE

I will do my part.

PRAYERFUL THOUGHTS

Dear Lord,

Teach me how to partner with my prayers.

Please guide me through the practical steps I should take.

Show what seeds to plant and what good habits to sow.

My heart is eager and willing.

In Jesus' name, amen.

KEEPSAKE

"In God's Kingdom, there are no excuses."

50. Not My Will

For Walking in Obedience

Small Green
Crested Flycatcher

ABOUT FIVE YEARS AGO, I had the opportunity to follow the deepest desire of my heart. It was a dream that I'd longed for since about the age of twelve. But after the opportunity presented itself, I didn't have peace. I sensed God asking me to say no.

Have there been days when I've questioned my decision to pass up that opportunity? *Yes! Absolutely! It was a lifelong dream!* But when we choose to obey the Lord, we win every time.

Disobedience is the primary reason our prayers are denied. What responsible parent would keep rewarding a disobedient child? In fact, the Bible states that Jesus became the King of kings and Lord of lords because he was *obedient.*

Philippians 2 says, "When he was living as a man, he humbled himself and was fully obedient to God. . . . So God raised him to the highest place. God made his name greater than every other name" (verses 8-9, NCV).

If we want our prayers answered, obedience is a must.

STRENGTH IN THE WORD

The LORD is watching everywhere, keeping his eyes on both the evil and the good.

PROVERBS 15:3

TODAY I DECLARE

I will walk in obedience.

PRAYERFUL THOUGHTS

Dear Lord,

Please forgive me for disobeying you. No one can fool you. You're the God who sees everything, even the buried sins of the heart.

Purify me, O Lord. I'm truly sorry for disobeying you. Reopen your ears to my prayers, and let me enter your presence again.

In Jesus' name, amen.

✻ KEEPSAKE

"Obedience is a must."

51. They Need It Most

For Our Enemies

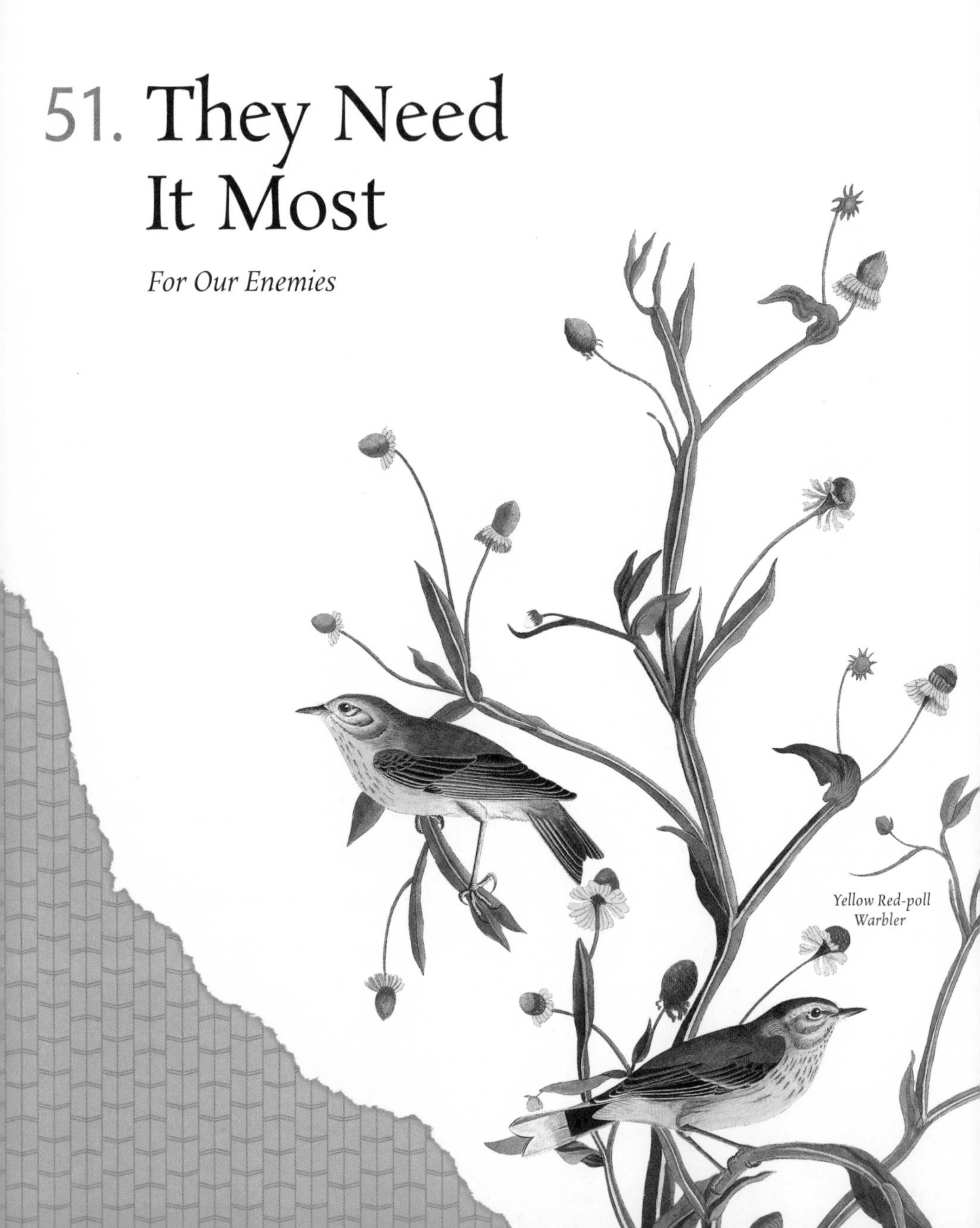

Yellow Red-poll Warbler

CALLED TO PRAY WOULD BE INCOMPLETE without a devotion on praying for our enemies. I must admit, this topic isn't one of my favorites. My carnal nature would prefer to ignore that part of Scripture. But that alone confirms its importance!

Let's be honest—praying for people who hurt and betray us isn't easy. But in Matthew 5:44-45, the Lord said, "I tell you to love your enemies and pray for anyone who mistreats you. Then you will be acting like your Father in heaven. He makes the sun rise on both good and bad people" (CEV).

That translation is especially powerful (and convicting) because it says we are to pray for "anyone." In essence God is asking us to climb one step higher than forgiveness; he wants us to use our prayers to *bless* even our worst enemy.

Therefore, as we pray for *our* peace, *our* patience, and *our* deliverance, let's also pray for the peace, patience, and deliverance of our enemies, for they need our prayers the most.

►◄ STRENGTH IN THE WORD

If your enemies are hungry, feed them. If they are thirsty, give them something to drink.

ROMANS 12:20

◄► TODAY I DECLARE

I'll pray for my enemies with a sincere heart.

PRAYERFUL THOUGHTS

Dear Lord,

This may be the hardest prayer to pray, but I know that it pleases you. And pleasing you, O Lord, is my greatest joy.

Please bless _______________, even though they've mistreated me. I'm praying that you send them peace, patience, and deliverance. Take away their pain, mend their broken pieces, and fill them with joy. Let your goodness and presence give them a change of heart.

In Jesus' name, amen.

KEEPSAKE

"They need our prayers the most."

52. It's Time

For Letting Go

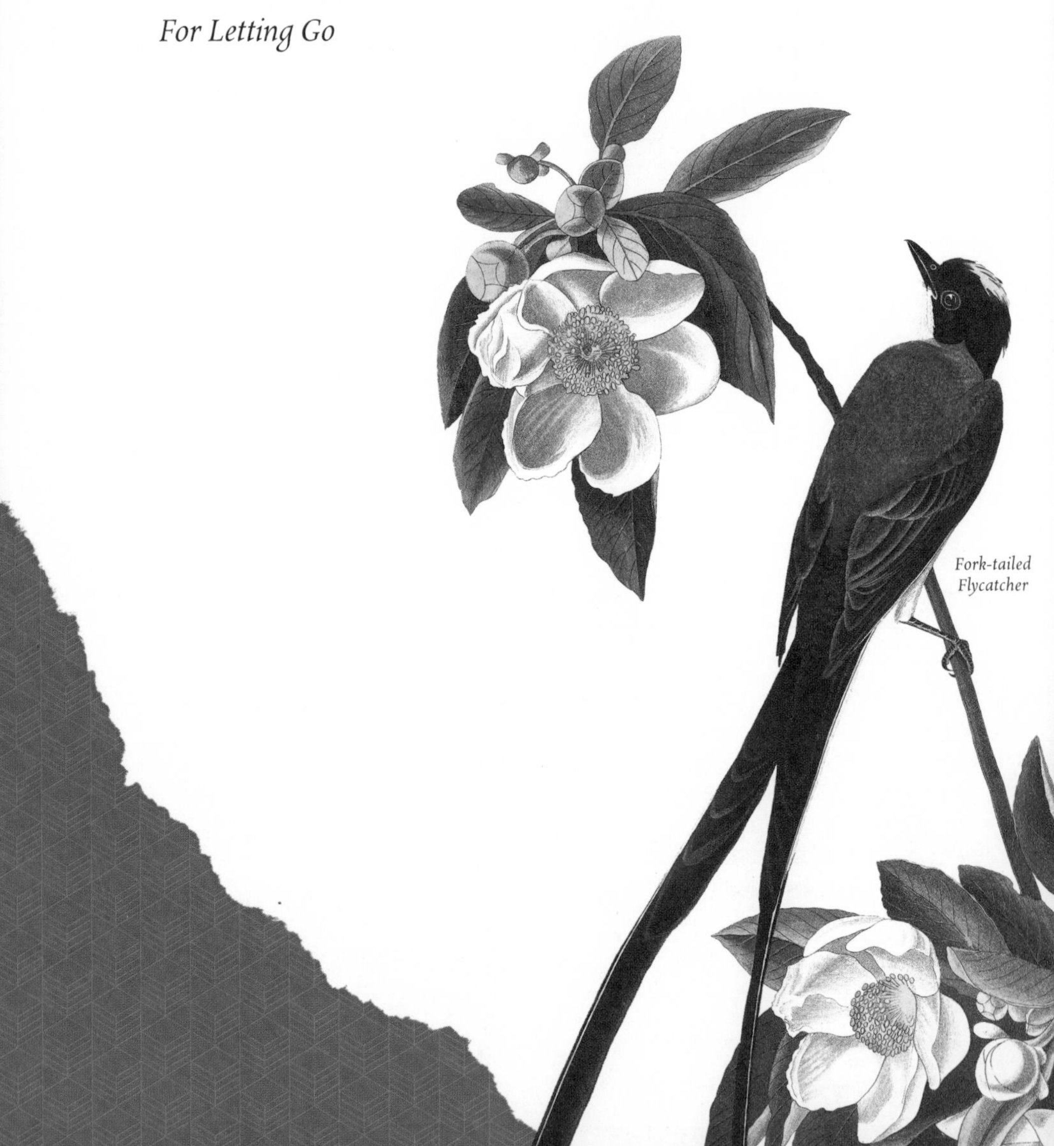

FOR SOME TIME, I've been fascinated with the weight limits set by airlines. I know that might sound strange, but the spiritual implications are glaring. If a plane is too heavy, it can't fly safely. And if our spirits are too loaded down, our lives are unable to soar.

God cares so much that he invites us to release our baggage in prayer. He is a load-bearing God. Psalm 55:22 encourages, "Give your burdens to the LORD, and he will take care of you." That includes the weight of our worries, regrets, shame, loneliness—*anything* that weighs us down.

Prayer is the unloading dock of our faith; it's where we exchange our burdens for God's rest. "Come to me, all you who are weary and burdened," Jesus said, "and I will give you rest. . . . For my yoke is easy and my burden is light" (Matthew 11:28, 30, NIV).

So, my sister, it's time to let the weight go. The Lord is asking that you give your heavy load to him.

STRENGTH IN THE WORD

They will soar on wings like eagles; they will run and not grow weary.

ISAIAH 40:31, NIV

TODAY I DECLARE

I release this load to God.

PRAYERFUL THOUGHTS

Dear Lord,

I feel overwhelmed. The weight of my burdens is too much to bear.

But you, O Lord, are my burden lifter. You have the strength to carry all loads. I release the baggage from my past, the stress of my present, and the worries I feel about my future. I'm releasing every burden to you. Please take it all, O Lord. Make my load light, and give me rest.

In Jesus' name, amen.

KEEPSAKE

"Prayer is the unloading dock of our faith."

NOTES

1. THE MEANING: FOR UNDERSTANDING PRAYER
You'll find 222 prayers in the King James Bible Finis J. Dake, *The Dake Annotated Reference Bible: KJV* (Laurens, SC: Dake Publishing, 1963). See "222 Prayers of the Bible," hopefaithprayer.com, https://www.hopefaithprayer.com/prayernew/222-prayers-of-the-bible/.

3. YOU ARE NOT ALONE: FOR ENDURING HARDSHIP
"Jesus has a very special love" Brian Kolodiejchuk, ed., *Mother Teresa: Come Be My Light* (New York: Doubleday, 2007), 288.

6. JUST SING: FOR PRAYING THROUGH SONGS
The book of Psalms is comprised Jeffrey Kranz, "All the Songs in the Bible [Infographic]," July 2, 2014, https://overviewbible.com/bible-songs/.

7. JESUS: FOR PRAYING HIS NAME
"When you don't know what else to pray" Clint Brown and Martha Munizzi, "Say the Name," copyright © 2002, Martha Munizzi Music.

10. GOOD VS. BEST: FOR WAITING ON GOD
The waiting list for this high-priced club Joanna Fantozzi, "This Is What It's Like to Eat at the Secret Club in Disneyland That Has a 14-Year Waiting List," *Insider*, August 24, 2017, https://www.insider.com/club-33-in-disneyland-review-2017-8.

14. YOUR UNIQUE APPROACH: FOR EXPLORING YOUR MINISTRY
"to preach the Gospel in patchwork" Lucine Finch, "A Sermon in Patchwork," *The Outlook*, October 1914.

16. JUST BECAUSE: FOR BUILDING FRIENDSHIP
"What a friend we have in Jesus" Lyrics by Joseph M. Scriven.

17. TELL ME WHO I AM: FOR SILENCING SELF-DOUBT
In one episode, it was revealed *The Crown*, season 2, episode 8, "Dear Mrs. Kennedy," directed by Stephen Daldry, written by Peter Morgan, Edward Hemming, and Laura Deeley, first aired December 8, 2017, on Netflix.

18. SEIZE THE OPPORTUNITY: FOR CHOOSING JOY
"around here . . . we don't look backwards" Walt Disney quote from the end credits of the 2007 computer-animated film *Meet the Robinsons*, which was produced by the Walt Disney Company.

21. "NO": FOR DENIED PRAYERS
Benjamin Morgan Palmer tells a compelling story B. M. Palmer, *Theology of Prayer* (Richmond, VA: Presbyterian Committee of Publication, 1894), 107–108.

24. VIEW IT DIFFERENTLY: FOR BENEFITING FROM REJECTION
the most exclusive journal in the world David Dobbs, "The Journal of Universal Rejection: Submit with Certainty," *WIRED*, January 28, 2011, https://www.wired.com/2011/01/the-journal-of-universal-rejection-submit-with-certainty/.

25. BE COURAGEOUS: FOR FACING FEAR
"The only thing we have to fear" Franklin Delano Roosevelt, "First Inaugural Address," March 3, 1933.

an extreme fear of fire Doris Kearns Goodwin, *No Ordinary Time* (New York: Simon & Schuster, 1994), 16.

27. FREE YOURSELF: FOR EMBRACING FORGIVENESS
"For a lot of years" Cliff Pinckard, "Ricky Jackson, Wrongly Imprisoned for 39 Years, Meets and Forgives Witness Who Helped Convict Him," Cleveland.com, January 6, 2015, https://www.cleveland.com/metro/2015/01/ricky_jackson_wrongly_imprison.html.

29. DON'T LET IT FESTER: FOR RELEASING GUILT
the United States Treasury has an official Conscience Fund Chris Weller, "There's a Place for Thieves with a Guilty Conscience to Return Money to the Government Anonymously," *Business Insider,* March 12, 2017, https://www.businessinsider.com/conscience-fund-us-treasury-2017-3.

33. ONE BODY: FOR UPLIFTING POLITICAL LEADERS
One day, the president paid a surprise visit Christine Szabo, "Pastor Expresses Sympathy for Church Members 'Hurt' by Surprise Trump Visit," ABC News, June 4, 2019, https://abcnews.go.com/Politics/pastor-expresses-sympathy-church-members-hurt-surprise-trump/story?id=63452430.

36. KEEP WATCH: FOR CONTROLLING YOUR THOUGHTS
nearly half of U.S. doctors Associated Press, "Half of U.S. Doctors Often Prescribe Placebos," NBC News, October 23, 2008, http://www.nbcnews.com/id/27342269/ns/health-health_care/t/half-us-doctors-often-prescribe-placebos/#.XjRDJ2hKiUk.

almost all U.K. physicians Michelle Roberts, "'Most Family Doctors' Have Given a Patient a Placebo Drug," BBC News, March 21, 2013, https://www.bbc.com/news/health-21834440.

40. FOCUS ON JESUS: FOR DISTRACTIONS
the average person spends more than five years "How We Waste Five Years of Our Lives Worrying about Issues Such as Money and Relationships," *Daily Mail,* January 27, 2013, https://www.dailymail.co.uk/news/article-2269291/How-waste-years-lives-worrying-issues-money-relationships.html.

42. JOYFUL OR PRICKLY: FOR AN ATTITUDE ADJUSTMENT
As the story goes David Mikkelson, "Who Are You?" Snopes, June 13, 2009, https://www.snopes.com/fact-check/who-are-you/.

43. BELIEVE AGAIN: FOR RESTORING HOPE
"I believe in the sun" Mark R. Lindsay, *Reading Auschwitz with Barth* (Cambridge, UK: James Clarke & Co., 2014), 131.

44. BE INTENTIONAL: FOR EXPRESSING GRATITUDE
we express thanks only 14.5 percent of the time Simeon Floyd et al., "Universals and Cultural Diversity in the Expression of Gratitude," *Royal Society Open Science* 5, no. 5, (May 1, 2018), https://royalsocietypublishing.org/doi/full/10.1098/rsos.180391.

45. CHERISH IT: APPRECIATING SMALL BEGINNINGS
The founders of the hospitality giant Airbnb Leigh Gallagher, "Airbnb's Surprising Path to Y Combinator," *WIRED,* February 21, 20117, https://www.wired.com/2017/02/airbnbs-surprising-path-to-y-combinator/.

47. REST AND INVEST: FOR SELF-LOVE
At the heart of what philosopher Kate Manne calls Julia Molony, "Tired but Wired: Why Are So Many of Us Suffering Burnout and What Can We Do about It?," *Irish Independent,* March 28, 2019, https://www.independent.ie/business/farming/rural-life/tired-but-wired-why-are-so-many-of-us-suffering-burnout-and-what-can-we-do-about-it-37960066.html.

49. ACTION IS REQUIRED: FOR ENDING EXCUSES
Itzhak Perlman fell in love Jean-Michel Molkhou, "About Itzhak Perlman," Warner Classics, https://www.warnerclassics.com/artist/itzhak-perlman.

ABOUT THE AUTHOR

MARSHA DuCILLE is the founder and editorial director of *CALLED* magazine, the largest North America–based publication for Christian women. Her "hobby turned global venture" reaches women worldwide through a variety of multimedia platforms. She is also the creative director of CALLED Design, a print and digital solutions enterprise; the creative principal of CALLED Boutique, a merchandising brand; and the chairman of The CALLED Project, a philanthropic arm that supports outreach efforts around the world. Marsha earned a master's degree in social work from Boston University and a master's degree in educational foundations, research, and policy from the University of Michigan.